Seeking the Light

A Quaker Journey for Quakers and Non-Quakers

Linda Seger, ThD

Praise for *Seeking the Light*

Linda Seger is serious about her Quaker faith. This book is a must-read for those who want to learn what Quaker faith is and how it's lived out. Seger's approach of including the experiences and practices of other Quakers in each chapter is not only unique but probably the most helpful way to accomplish that. Quakerism is as much a movement as it is a specific church faith, so to describe it through the experiences of a number of faithful Quakers provides a thorough and moving picture. Spiritual experience and faithful practice lie at the heart of the Quaker faith and Seger has captured both succinctly in this book.

~Bill and Genie Durland
Quaker authors and activists

When my longtime friend Dr. Linda Seger lived in Los Angeles, we used to have fascinating face-to-face conversations about her Quaker spiritual practice and my Jewish spiritual practice. Now she is in Colorado and I loved reading her new book

Seeking the Light, which not only describes Quaker values but can also deepen all of our explorations of the mysterious silence, the light, the importance of community, and the search for healing and repair that are found in each of our spiritual traditions. This book is very profound and inspiring.

~Len Felder, PhD, author of *The Ten Challenges* and *How These Words Can Raise Up Your Energy*

I love Linda Seger's new book, *Seeking the Light*. The book is readable, moving, and it cuts through Quaker jargon. I recommend that both Quakers—especially newcomers—and people who aren't Quakers read it and deepen their spiritual lives. The intense explorations about the metaphors associated with the Light stun me.

~Stanford J. Searl, Jr., Ph.D, Quaker scholar, poet, and author

Reading Linda Seger's book *Seeking the Light* was more than a pleasure. It inspired me, challenged me, and reminded me why I love Linda so much! I not only learned what being a Quaker really is, but

I love what Quakers live for! Linda lives out every concept in this book and her beautiful, peaceful, giving, loving heart is on every page! Coming from a Catholic upbringing, to becoming an Evangelical Christian in college, and then becoming a producer in Hollywood and running a non-denominational Prayer ministry, I relate to everything Linda writes. I have learned about the rich background and foundation of Quakers, I have seen through Linda's poignant stories, beautiful examples of these "testimonies," and I am inspired to live out more intentionally the tenets of her faith. I am excited to buy this book for family members and friends as a source of great inspiration! So, AMEN to seeking the Light, spending time in silence and living lives of simplicity, peace, integrity, community, equality and stewardship. Thank you Linda for making me feel even closer to God. I believe the world will be a better place because of this book!

~Karen Covell, Producer and
Founding Director of The
Hollywood Prayer Network

The cheerful descriptions of Quaker faith make our weirdnesses seem more accessible. There is much in this book to help newcomers understand Quaker silent worship.

~Signe Wilkinson, Quaker,
Pulitzer Prize winning cartoonist

Seeking the Light:

A Quaker Journey for Quakers and Non-Quakers

Softcover ISBN: 978-1-7377982-5-5

Published in the United States 2022 by Red Typewriter Press, P.O. Box 535, Cascade, CO 80809.

Cover design by: Nick Zelinger: http://nzgraphics.com.

Cover photograph: Chattanooga Friends Meeting in Chattanooga, Tennessee, photographed by Ben Schnell: www.chattanoogafriendsmeeting.org.

Interior design by: Carmen Barber: KeepingYouWriting@gmail.com.

Table of Contents

Acknowledgments xi

Introduction: Who are the Quakers? 15

Part 1: Our Faith and Our Practice 39

Chapter 1: Seeking the Light 41

Chapter 2: Sitting in Silence 79

The SPICES 107

PART 2: The Testimonies.................. 115

Chapter 3: The Simplicity Testimony 117

Chapter 4: The Peace Testimony 143

Chapter 5: The Integrity Testimony 181

Chapter 6: The Community Testimony.. 219

Chapter 7: The Equality Testimony...... 257

Chapter 8: The Stewardship Testimony.. 285

Final Thoughts............................. 315

Notes 321

About the Author........................... 326

Other Books by Dr. Linda Seger 328

Dedicated to the Portland (Maine) Friends Meeting Daily Worship Group:

Dennis, Diana, Hope, Jamie,
Karyl, Maggie, Peter, Rhoda,
Shannon, Stan, Sydney, Mey, Dee
Francis, Lyn, and Chris.

Acknowledgments

Thank you:

To my assistant, Heidi Bailey, who has helped me through the writing of this book, from beginning to end. She has typed the whole book, given me feedback, and stayed with me through all the delays of my illness throughout the writing of most of this book. Her commitment and care has been extraordinary!

To my editor, Carmen Barber, who also has formatted the book and then put it on Amazon when it was ready. Her understanding, and thoroughness, always impresses me. Thanks also to Marjorie Vawter for her proofreading and editing assistance.

To my cover designer, Nick Zelinger, for his amazing talent and commitment to find the right cover for each of my books. He doesn't give up and I'm so appreciative of how his creative process blends with my creative process.

To my readers who gave me such important feedback: Lynn Lee, Cathleen Loeser, Lindsay Smith, and Diana White.

To all who assisted me or sent me quotes about their Quaker experiences:

> Diana White, Dennis Redfield, Maggie Fehr, Shannon O'Connor, Lyn Ballou, Beth Bussiere—Portland, Maine Friends Meeting;
>
> Sara Primo, Mary Tracy—Portland, Maine Friends School;
>
> Cathleen Loeser, Stan Searle—Santa Monica Friends Meeting;
>
> Bill and Genie Durland—Mountain View Friends Meeting, Denver;
>
> Migs Eder, Murray Short and Derek Carver—Christchurch, New Zealand Friends Meeting;
>
> Carlton Gamer, Ann Grant Martin, Nancy Andrew—Colorado Springs Friends Meeting;

Ginger Morgan—Madison, Wisconsin Friends Meeting;

Trevor Bending and Jan Arriens—Quaker Truth and Integrity Group, Great Britain;

Patricia Johnson—Cannon Valley Friends Meeting, Minnesota;

Gregory and Ruth Heath—Concord, New Hampshire Friends Meeting.

Thank you to Colonel Lynn Lee for her insights for the Peace Chapter.

Thank you to Chattanooga Friends Meeting for their permission to use the photo on the cover. Larry and Ben, I am so thankful for your help and for the amazing photograph!

And always, thank you to my dear husband, Peter Le Var, who is always by my side encouraging me, cheering me on, supporting me, reading chapters, and always believes in me.

Introduction: Who are the Quakers?

Margaret Fell (1624–1691)
Mother of Quakerism

George Fox (1614–1702)
Founder of Religious Society of Friends (Quakers)

The Religious Society of Friends, also referred to as the Quaker Movement, was founded in England in the 17th century by George Fox. He and other early Quakers [such as Margaret Fell—sometimes called the Mother of Quakerism] . . . were persecuted for their beliefs, which included the idea that the presence of God exists in every person. Quakers rejected elaborate religious ceremonies, didn't have official clergy, and believed in spiritual equality for men and women . . . Quakers, who practice pacifism, played a key role in both the abolitionist, and women's rights movements.

History.com

Our life is love, and peace, and tenderness.

Isaac Penington (1616–1679)

You've probably heard about Quakers. You might be a Quaker, or you might be intrigued enough to open this book and wonder what we're all about.

If you don't know much about Quakers, you might think of the fellow on the Quaker™ Oatmeal box. The Quaker character was chosen by a non-Quaker manufacturer because he wanted his product to represent the values of integrity, honesty, and purity, which were known as Quaker values.

Some of you may have a vague memory of the 1956 film, *Friendly Persuasion,* based on the 1945 book by Jessamyn West. If you've seen the movie, you may remember it dealt with how the American Civil War tested a Quaker family's pacifist beliefs. The family must confront themselves, each other, and their Quaker community as they struggle with the demands of war and peace. You might start humming the theme song, "Thee I Love." Perhaps you might trip a little bit over the "thees" and "thous," which were used by Quakers in earlier times.

People often confuse the Amish, Mennonites, and even the Mormons with Quakers. Once, while flying cross-country, I mentioned I was a Quaker to my seatmate. He screwed up his eyebrows as he searched for what he knew or thought he knew about Quakers. A light of realization flashed across his face and he said, "Oh, you're the people who had to put tail lights on their buggies." I gently explained that those were the Amish, but gave him credit for trying, as I silently thought of the humor of flying in a 747 airplane, miles above buggies with taillights, and of his determination to show that he understood.

If some of you reading this book know me as a writer, colleague, associate, or friend, you know more about Quakerism than you realize. I'm a Quaker, and I've been one since 1970. I have expressed my Quaker values and beliefs through personal and professional decisions, and found they have guided me and enriched me in many profound ways.

You Might Know Something of Our History

You might have heard of George Fox who founded Quakerism in the 1600s. Perhaps you've heard of William Penn, an English Quaker who founded the state of Pennsylvania. Some of the first abolitionists were Quakers, beginning as early as the 1600s, including John Woolman in the 1700s and the poet John Greenleaf Whittier from the 1800s.

Many of the early feminist activists were Quakers, including Susan B. Anthony, the Grimké sisters, Lucretia Coffin Mott, and Alice Paul, who was a suffragette in the forefront of women's right to vote in 1919 and co-authored the Equal Rights Amendment.

Some of our greatest actors are Quakers. These include: Judi Dench, F. Murray Abraham, and James Dean, who was raised as a Quaker. Tyne Daley, known for the television series *Cagney and Lacey*, attended the Santa Monica Meeting after playing a Quaker character in the TV series *Christy*. Other famous Quakers include author James Michener; philanthropist Johns Hopkins; musicians Bonnie Raitt and Joan Baez; and John Cadbury, who founded the chocolate company bearing his name in 1824. The two Quaker U.S. presidents, who were not known for their adherence to Quaker values, were Richard Nixon and Herbert Hoover.

The American Friends Service Committee was honored with a Nobel Peace Prize in 1947. The Nobel Committee awarded it to them "for their pioneering work in the international peace movement and their compassionate effort to relieve human suffering, thereby promoting the fraternity between nations." The Quakers were recognized for their peace work during many wars—ever since Quakers began—but especially for peace work they did during two World Wars, from 1914 to 1945.

What Do Others Think About Us?

Often, when I mention that I'm a Quaker, people respond with a certain respect, even though they may know little about us. Their response often surprises me because I expect them to say, "What's that?" But whatever they have heard about Quakers seems to have been positive. They almost naturally fall into a moment of reflection as if entering into the quiet spirit of our denomination. Quakers are often described as peaceful, honest, trustworthy, unassuming, and hard-working. They are known as tenderhearted and gentle folk.

Years ago, I attended a Christian Gala and sat down next to an older couple. I knew that many of the people at this dinner were Conservatives and Evangelicals, so I asked the couple what church they attended. "We're Southern Baptists," they replied and asked for my denomination. I answered "Quaker" and wondered how they would respond. Quakers tend to be progressive and different than usual church folk in terms of our outlook and worship. I expected the woman to either know nothing about

Quakers or to feel we were not Christian enough. Her reply surprised me. She took a deep breath and said in a hushed tone, "Oh, I heard the Quaker, Elton Trueblood, speak once." He is considered one of the foremost Quaker writers and theologians. She continued, speaking slowly and more softly than she had spoken a moment before. "There was a Silent Meeting that followed his speech."

Silent Meetings are the Quaker form of worship. We don't have ministers. We sit in silence. If someone is moved by the Spirit to speak, they share a short message of three to five minutes then sit down, and we move back into silence. I wondered how a Baptist with their many songs and sometimes rousing services would respond to a Quaker Meeting. Her answer was not what I expected: "That was one of the most spiritual experiences I have ever had." She paused. "That is such a beautiful religion."

A few years after I became a Quaker, I began studying the relationship of spirituality and creativity, which became my life's work. I once read an interview by a psychological researcher who was exploring how an individual's religion affected their art. He had interviewed a Methodist and an Episcopalian artist, among others, and gave an objective, factual report about what they said. He then interviewed a Quaker artist and the tone of the interview changed. There was an emotional, subjective component that had not been present in the others. The researcher struggled to find the right words to describe what seemed different about this artist. He noticed that the way she described her creative process was more reflective than the others, as if she was reaching deep inside herself, expressing herself honestly, slowly, and deliberately. The interviewer talked about how authentic she was. It left him with a sense of awe.

I noticed in these responses there was a reflective hush in the way each person spoke about these interactions, as if something from the Quakers had rubbed off on them.

My First Knowledge of Quakers

I was twelve years old the first time I heard about Quakers. My family was going on a vacation to Washington, D.C., on a train. My mother had left her seat to take a train walk and she came back about an hour later, intrigued by a young Quaker woman she had met. Mom started to talk in a slow and thoughtful way about their conversation regarding this woman's faith. Mother had an immediate respect for this woman, and her reaction to their conversation was more reflective than was usual for her. We had certainly met many people in our lives, and my mother's usual response was one of excitement and fascination by the new knowledge she had gained. Mom was not by nature a quiet, introspective person. Somehow this conversation slowed her down.

When my mom said this woman was not a Christian, but rather a Quaker, I began to feel threatened. I was deep into my self-righteous stage of determining which religions and denominations were okay and which ones were not, and I knew little about non-Christians at that age. I grew up Lutheran and came from a long line of Lutheran ministers, missionaries, and theologians.

I grew up with stained-glass windows in the church with familiar themes—Jesus in the Garden of Gethsemane and Jesus the Good Shepherd. Lots of hymns with my mother playing the organ and leading the choir. Scripture—always the Old Testament lesson, the Gospel reading, and the reading from the Epistles. And music—much of it beautiful, some quite staid. Sermons and prayers for every occasion, including a very long prayer at the end of the service that covered just about everything.

I was an intolerant young girl in my little mainstream Protestant bubble, and I didn't know how to think about Mother's encounter and her reaction.

Some years later, I learned there are many Quakers who are Christian and many who are not, even though our historical roots are Christian. I'm a Christian Quaker, while other Quakers identify with religions such as Jewish Quakers, Buddhist Quakers, and other combinations. And there are Quakers who feel no need to connect with another religion. We believe the Holy Spirit is universal and does not have denominational preferences.

Why I Became a Quaker

In 1969, I was teaching at a Southern Baptist College in Phoenix, Arizona—Grand Canyon College. I had not yet found a denomination that was fulfilling my needs, and I decided to go church shopping. I had gone to many churches on the religious continuum, and had also studied religions of the world. After those studies, I decided to remain Christian. I recalled Mother's reaction to the Quaker woman on the train and decided to check out a Quaker Meeting, which was last on my list. I knew I had to deepen my spiritual life. It was time to balance my extroversion with some introspection. I needed to be more reflective. I needed to bring harmony to my inner life. I was seeking to become more tolerant and less judgmental. I wanted to smooth out my metaphorical wrinkles and many of the bumpy parts of my personality and my spirituality. I was bubbly and extroverted with a thousand ideas running through my mind even as a young child. I had clear boundaries and drew clear lines and was capable of judging just about everything. By my early twenties, I was self-righteous and a bit insufferable. But like many of us, I was looking for a Center. I was seeking a place where the Holy Spirit could be nurtured and grown within me. I sat down in my first Quaker Meeting. I was home.

Maybe at heart, we are all seeking peace at the Center of our being. We are seeking something that overcomes those forces of greed and power and might that can so often rule us. We are drawn into one life and have difficulty seeing the possibilities of a life that is more centered and tranquil and peaceful.

Over my fifty-plus years as a Quaker, I have gained more and more faith in Quaker processes and the workings of the Holy Spirit, which I share in this book. I've often found non-Quakers as well are drawn to Quaker ideas and practices.

Is Quakerism Practical?

Any religion or denomination can be moral, uplifting, inspirational, and can nurture the Spirit within. Different religions focus on different aspects of belief, faith, spiritual experience, and how to integrate particular principles into our personal and professional lives.

Many Christian denominations focus on belief systems. They have statements of faith and dogmas and in some cases, a list of what people should believe in order to be part of that church. Instead, Quakers use the phrase, "But what do you say? What is your experience of the Holy Spirit? How do you find God working in your life? Do you feel moved, inspired, transformed by Something or Someone or a Presence that guides you? How does this Presence make you a better person and the world a better place?"

Quakers look to experience, believing that this Spirit is universal and accessible to everyone, regardless of religion or creed. Our values and testimonies have an inner movement that then expresses itself outwardly in our family lives, our professional lives, and our commitment to social justice. Certainly, many of us have belief systems and philosophies, but we hope they take root in our inner life and also have an impact in our world.

I began my career as a college drama teacher. When job opportunities closed down and I lived near Los Angeles, I decided to move from theater into film. I thought it would be a natural and easy process, but it wasn't. One of the problems was my age. I was already in my thirties, and many executives wanted to hire assistants in their twenties. Many executives considered me "over educated" because I already had two M.A. degrees (one in Drama and one in Religion and the Arts) and a ThD (in Drama and Theology). The film business is a practical business, and in 1979, any education past a bachelor's degree was considered too scholarly to be practical. I analyzed what skill I had that the film industry might want. They needed typists, and I was a really fast one. I removed all the degrees from my resume except my B.A. in

English and sold myself on my typing skills and my ability to analyze scripts.

I entered the film industry in 1979, working as an assistant to the assistant of the Director of Development at Norman Lear's company. On the side, I did freelance work as a script reader, sometimes called a story analyst. As a reader, I reviewed scripts and books, wrote a two- or three-page synopsis of the story, and then a paragraph or two about whether it should be considered for possible production. In most cases, the submissions had many problems and I only recommended about one out of every twenty-five scripts. In 1981, after losing my job because of a writer's strike, I started a part-time script consulting business based on my doctoral dissertation project which included an analysis of what elements make up a great drama. I saw a need for screenwriters to have an objective, professional analysis that could help them identify script problems which needed to be solved in the rewrite stage.

Over a four-year period, my business began to grow. With success came a series of spiritual challenges. I decided I would try to integrate my Christian faith and Quaker practice into all parts of my career. In the film industry, as is true in many businesses, temptations abound to fudge, lie, not speak up, get angry and frustrated, and find ways to benefit ourselves, and sometimes to harm others. Egos abound—and certainly many of us in the film business have no lack of ego. Often, we puff ourselves up and think far too highly of ourselves. Other times, we compare ourselves to others and find we come up short. We can then become self-deprecating and demean ourselves. Sometimes we work against each other, tearing others down in hopes of building ourselves up.

Perhaps no industry is more seductive and enchanting than the entertainment industry. It is a minefield of greed, ambition, favoritism and nepotism, passion, elation and disappointment, networking, integrity and inauthenticity, stargazing, and insecurity.

And yet, the film industry can be a business of collaboration and teamwork leading to extraordinary art. Sometimes the kindness and support of colleagues is unexpectedly generous. Yes, everything you've heard about it is true—the good and the bad. I believe I have survived and thrived, partly because I lived as a Quaker in the midst of this business.

I presumed that by following spiritual practices in my business, I would not do as well as others financially, but I also believed I would be taken care of by God and would be all right since I believed this was my calling. There is a Quaker saying, "They came to do good and ended up doing well." That was historically true for many Quaker merchants, and it was eventually true for me as I discovered I could be successful and fulfilled without compromising my spiritual values. I discovered that good, ethical practices ripple outwards and ripple back.

I began to confront my own feelings of competition and change my attitude toward others in my field. I decided that instead of having competitors, I would have colleagues Anybody who had a goal of making better films was on my side, and I was on their side. One of my colleagues once wrote an article declaring war on me and another well-known colleague, because he felt our concepts about screenwriting were wrong. I was told that I had the right to respond and that the magazine would publish my response in defense. I titled my article, "Linda Seger Declares Peace: We're on the Same Side." This shift in thinking took me about ten years of prayer and attitude adjustment, but I was determined to not live my life with these negative attitudes toward others.

What Is This Book About?

This book is not a memoir. Nor is it a history of Quakerism. It is an exploration of eight different aspects of Quakerism that are both moral and practical. These values can be applied and integrated into our lives whether we are Quakers or not. If you're a Quaker, hopefully this will deepen your faith as you learn how other contemporary Quakers apply their faith to their daily lives. If you are not a Quaker, hopefully you will find many ways that your own spiritual life can be enriched by integrating some of these ideas and values. Sometimes I will refer to my work within the film business, since that is where I spent forty years.

Every occupation—be it hard-hat labor, teaching, parenting, running a company, or running a country—is layered with challenges and choices. Every industry has its unique character, where we have to confront how we keep a Center in the midst of temptations. I believe a little bit of Quakerism—or a lot of it—can rub off and provide a ballast against the many tempests that impact our lives.

While writing this book, I gathered ideas from a small team of Quakers from various Meetings in the United States, Great Britain, and New Zealand. Although I mention certain historical figures and parts of Quaker history, this book focuses on how contemporary Quakers are living out their faith in our modern world. These are people you would not have heard of. They are not famous and well-known or best-selling authors or leaders of religious groups. They are ordinary Quakers. They will be referred to by their first name in most instances, but I am including their first and last names in the acknowledgments as well as mentioning their Quaker Meeting.

Life is fraught with difficult individual decisions and even social, political, and religious dilemmas. How we live our lives, walking on whatever path we are on, is a subject Quakerism addresses.

Can Anyone Adopt Quaker Values?

I write this book because I believe Quaker values and spirituality can enrich anyone's spiritual and daily life.

This is not a book about conversion. Quakers believe in encouraging others to find their own paths and to embrace whatever expands their own spirituality. We are always open to people wandering into one of our Meetings and staying for a time, or forever, but Quakers on the whole, do not proselytize. There is a branch of Quakerism called the Friend's Church, which is much like a traditional denomination and tends to be evangelical, but this book is written from the point of view of the Unprogrammed Friends Meeting, a silent Meeting without ministers.

Many of you may be seeking the Centering Peace, that Presence which is at the core of our existence. Many of you may be seeking inspiration and methods for navigating the challenges you face. You do not need to be a Quaker to practice Quaker values and actions. I hope the ideas in this book will draw you inward and expand you outward. Perhaps you will find these ideas fascinating, just as my mother did when she met that Quaker woman on the train so many years ago.

Queries

Quakers use queries to help them reflect on their own spiritual lives. These queries invite us to examine what we are doing and where we fall short. They often lead us to decisions, transformations, and commitments to action. They affirm our Quaker values and challenge us to live by those values and testimonies. To assist you with your own journey, each chapter will end with queries.

When did you first hear about Quakers?

What was your immediate attitude toward Quakers?

What is mentioned in this introduction that makes you interested in reading this book?

Part 1:
Our Faith and Our Practice

Chapter 1:
Seeking the Light

Presence in the Midst[1]

Quakers, members of the Religious Society of Friends, believe that in every person there is 'that of God' which acts as an Inner Guide or teacher, sometimes called The Light Within or the Inner Light.

BUCKINGHAM FRIENDS SCHOOL, PENNSYLVANIA[2]

But, dear friends, mind the Light of God . . . which . . . dwelling in it, guides out of the many things into one spirit.

George Fox, Founder of Quakerism, 1624–1691[3]

All of us, and I say this with some certainty, have experienced the Light that seems to permeate all of humanity and all of our world. We have been on the giving and the receiving end of kindness, love, mercy, compassion, and generosity. Although this Light might have been a glimmer rather than that bright light that warms us and enlivens us, its presence is a fact of life. When God breathed life into Adam—however you understand that story—something happened. It wasn't mere physical life that bloomed.

Those of us who grew up in a church, and those who became Quakers, are often quite comfortable with traditional names that describe this Light. In the Bible, there are about three hundred words for God and Christ and the Holy Spirit—such as Yahweh, Savior, Healer, Lord, the Light of the World, the Messiah, Jesus, and Son of God. In Islam there are ninety-nine words for God, some of them similar or the same as in Judaism and Christianity. These include the Creator, the Preserver, the Merciful, the All Seeing. Quakers use some of the same words since our faith is rooted in scripture as well. These references to Light can be found throughout the Bible.

Some of these definitions come from the Gospel of John which describe Jesus as the Light of the World who overcomes the darkness (John 1:5), who enlightens everyone (John 1:9). Quakers sometimes use the words "The Seed," "The Christ Within," "The Source," "The Truth," "The Presence," "The Sacred," "The Divine Light," "The Light Within," or "The Inner Light." Most of these words, which come from different religions and different spiritual practices, seek to define the sacred and this Most Holy Spirit who is both immanent and transcendent.

The Historical Understanding of Light

In the seventeenth century, George Fox founded Quakerism as a community of believers who believed that everyone was able to experience and be led by the Light of God. This was quite a different belief than the churches of his time, which believed that the priest or the minister was the intercessor and the authority figure and stood between the people and God. Church leaders did not believe that the common folk were capable of interpreting the Bible or had direct access to our Creator. Quaker theology was considered highly heretical and, of course, could put certain authorities out of jobs. It also put a huge responsibility on those who believed they had access directly to God. How did they know that what they were interpreting was truly from God and not from the devil?

Quakers tried to deal with this important question in two different ways. Although they didn't believe that the Bible was literally true with every word of the translation, they did believe that it was an inspired document and they studiously studied the scriptures, memorized them, and took scriptural moral authority very seriously. They believed that their interpretation of the Light would not contradict the scriptures. They also believed in pondering and reflecting carefully on the guidance of the Light. They sat in silence together and shared their experiences and messages, at times relying on each other's wisdom to keep them in check. They did not make decisions quickly. When they felt they had received a message from this Inner Light, they sat with this message for a while—sometimes for a day or a month or a year or more.

Finding Our Way

Many of us who grew up in a religious setting find we need to unpack the words that are laden with centuries of meaning, but now sometimes get in our way because they are no longer relevant to our religious thinking. I no longer think of God as the Mighty Fortress, although I respect Martin Luther who wrote this hymn. For some, God as the Father seems limited since it leaves out the nurturing and nourishing motherly qualities of God in the Bible which describes God as a mother (Psalm 131:2), a mother hen (Matthew 23:37, Luke 13:34), a mother eagle (Deuteronomy 32:11–12), or a woman who is the finder of the lost coin (Luke 15:8–10).

Not all Quakers believe in the Trinity and see God as Unity; however, I still find the Trinity image expanding and dimensional.

Maggie from Portland, Maine, says:

> I grew up as a Catholic. The Trinity—Father, Son, and Holy Ghost—was a very important aspect of the religion. But from early on, even as a child, I was afraid of God and Jesus and the Holy Ghost (which to me was just a ghost for Halloween). Later, when I came to Quakerism, I began to see the Holy Ghost as the Holy Spirit, and then as the Spirit that leads me and helps me make it through hard times. The Spirit is in the Light. Instead of fear, I learned to see the Spirit as warm and loving.

Quakers believe "there is that of God in everyone," in spite of some evidence to the contrary. This informs their relationship with the Divine Within as well as the God that is within others.

Diana from Portland, Maine, says:

> There is no outer God, extant as a separate powerful entity. I like the expression that we are 'the Divine's hands,' because it is our deeds and words that create a moral and just world.

We believe and have faith that the darkness cannot ever totally overcome the Light. The Light might be a small spark or a glimmer or the eternal flame. At times, this Light is easily accessible, and at other times it's an ember struggling to hold on to the tiniest flicker.

No matter the situation—whether a big crisis or a small one, whether there is the need for direction, whether the desire is to find a better path—the Light is always there as a guide and a comfort. Quakers have a saying, "Follow the Light you have," and we recognize that we don't always have the Light we want, but we always have some small ray. They also have a saying, "As the Way opens," meaning if there is only a little light leading us, we try to step out with trust and faith and courage, not always knowing where it is leading us. We train ourselves to seek the Light, to pay attention to what the Light shows us.

One of my favorite quotes was said in a sermon when I graduated from seminary. The president of the seminary told my graduating class, "You know you're on the way to the Promised Land by the fear that you feel when you take the first step." Many of us who try to follow a Leading, which is sometimes much like the religious term "a Calling," know that fear is part of the process. We have to discern whether the fear is telling us to be cautious and not take the risk, or whether the fear is telling us that it's important we step forward. That takes a certain amount of training ourselves and being willing to read, discuss, and turn to others for help to figure out how to understand how this Inner Light is working within us.

Experiencing the Light

Quakers often ask the question, "What do you know experientially?" Other religions might ask "What do you believe?" and "Who do you follow?" Some religions might ask for a statement of faith or clarity about the dogma that their followers believe. Some churches will have individuals sign on to this statement in order to become members.

Quakers believe that we can experience this relationship with the Divine, and that it is immediate and present if we but listen. Quakers put emphasis on listening rather than talking. We see our faith and practice begins with paying attention to what is going on in our own spiritual seeking and preparing to follow where that leads.

In the early 1980s, I was asked to be clerk of the Santa Monica Friends Meeting. As part of my preparation for this responsibility, I wanted to talk to a spiritual director and wrote a letter to one of the foremost

Quaker theologians, Elton Trueblood. I asked whether he might be willing to talk to me as a spiritual advisor or if he knew an experienced Quaker who would talk to me. We don't have spiritual directors in the way that Catholics have, but there are certainly many wise Quakers who we call Elders—meaning they have been Quakers for a long time and have wisdom and insights and the ability to lead. He recommended a woman named Barbara Graves who lived in San Francisco. I called Barbara and told her Elton Trueblood recommended her as a possible spiritual director for me. She gave a humble laugh and then agreed to see me. The first question she asked was: "What do you know about your soul?" What a profound question that was! I realized I knew quite a bit about my soul. I knew something about what nurtured it. I knew about bad decisions and good decisions. I knew about times when I felt a path unfolding and took that path. Other times, I turned away because of fear and uncertainty.

I knew something about Truth and Integrity and how difficult it is sometimes to hold to what we know to be true because of all the resistances that can knock us off our tracks.

I knew something about my confusions. And I knew about times that my soul took me on a less conventional path, and I somehow had the courage to follow it.

From my seminary training and growing up in a church, I was already reading the Bible daily and was familiar with the statements of faith and dogmas of several different denominations. Sometimes I encountered religious judgments that did not sit well with my soul. And often there were good reasons to question these judgments.

Barbara helped me trust the Light I had experienced and that had guided me well to this point in my life. She encouraged me to trust the God that I knew experientially and to continue to follow the Good and the Truth. And she gave an extra push for me to continue to seek the Light in all aspects of my life.

What Does the Light Do? The Light Can Soften the Edges

We all have some conflicts along the way of life with people who either rub us the wrong way, do us wrong, deceive us, betray us, get under our skin, goad us, don't appreciate us, or make our lives miserable with their toxicity. The temptation is to rage against them, belittle them, blame them, demean them, or ignore them. We might even deny the truth about the terrible impact this negativity can have if we don't confront it in one way or another.

Instead of joy, there can be despair. Instead of peace, there can be a pit in our stomach that simply will not go away and seems to endure for days or weeks or years. What is to be done about the negative part of human existence?

Quakers try to hold these people and these issues up to the Light. Whereas others might do this through prayer—and Quakers do pray—Quakers might imagine the Light enveloping this person. Sitting in silence and allowing the Light to do its sacred work can lead to peace, calm us down, and ease the irritations. It might help us see more clearly and recognize that maybe this other person is struggling. Maybe the Light shows us this person doesn't have the skill-set to deal with the problem. Maybe they're enraged because of oppressions and repressions and suppressions that have been done to them that are not their fault. Maybe they had a difficult childhood or are having a bad adulthood and it's taken its toll on their ability to let their good side shine through. Simply gaining a new understanding and empathy can go a long way to soften irritations.

Sometimes the Light helps us recognize we are holding on to our own righteousness. If we stop blaming the other person, maybe it means that we stop believing that we are the one who is in the right. This seems to be counter to our understanding of the Truth. If we can't tell right from wrong and if we can't name it, then are we just letting the other person off the hook without accountability or responsibility? Yet, when we hold a person or an issue up to the Light, we often recognize we are asking the wrong questions and are concerned about the wrong issue. Suddenly we get a little softer inside. We might decide that we don't have all the answers and don't even need to. We can be truthful with ourselves. We can be firm with the other person without holding a grudge. We can stand on our integrity. And at the very same time, we learn that we can be merciful and give the other person a break. The Light can take us to a quiet place where metal no longer rubs against metal, and all is well in spite of difficult circumstances. Our raw edges have been embraced and honed, which gives us the ability to embrace the human nature of the other.

This can lead to us making amends or asking for forgiveness or apologizing for our own role in the conflict. Or it can lead us to walking away from a situation that we know is not going to improve. But we don't need to carry the bad feelings with us because that Light within has made us calm again.

What Does the Light Do? The Light can Reveal Our Integrity

We sometimes struggle and ask the question: "If we compromise, are we also compromising our integrity? How do we speak our truth without drawing a line in the sand or making the other person wrong?"

We wonder: "Can we be firm and diplomatic and kind without denying our own value system or pretending it doesn't matter?"

Some years ago, I was in a difficult situation and had to decide whether to leave an organization I loved. I tried to resolve the conflict through a number of different means but was not getting anywhere. The pit in my stomach remained and I knew I had not yet found the peace of resolution. I decided to seek the advice of a Catholic spiritual director who I have occasionally seen for many years and is very respectful of me as a Quaker. She clarified the problem by telling me, "Your integrity will not allow you to stay in a situation that is hurting you or abusing you or offending you." She encouraged me to recognize that it was all right to disengage. She also encouraged me to continue to take my feelings seriously. She said, "When we feel hurt or insulted or offended, perhaps there is something going on that is harmful to us, and rather than denying it or learning to live with it or deciding it is my problem rather than a bigger problem, we instead value the insight." The Light can work through our emotional experiences. It can lead us to recognize when something isn't working for us experientially.

It can help us see when a person or an organization is asking us to compromise the truth we know. Our integrity might be asking us to take a different path and the Light leads us to the next step.

What Does the Light Do?
The Light Can Recognize Deception

I had a script-consulting business for almost forty years, and I sometimes worked with dishonest people. Often, I didn't recognize deception because it wasn't part of my background. It took me some experiences and some wisdom to begin to admit that there are dishonest people who will lie and cheat. I always struggled with that fine line between letting something go, and recognizing that dishonesty needed to be called out—perhaps diplomatically. I needed to understand when somebody else's dishonesty was eating away at me and not getting resolved. I also needed to recognize when someone else's dishonesty was hurting others as well as myself.

Quakers often create queries to help them reflect on these issues that need Light. In a situation like this, they might ask: "When do we disconnect and disengage, and when do we stick it out because there is an issue of Justice or Truth? How do we confront dishonesty from our own integrity, rather than from a sense of judgment and mean spiritedness? How long do we wait for someone to make amends for a wrong and make things right? At what point do we actually give up on that other person and walk away? How do we assess the human nature of someone who abuses us? At what point do we recognize the truth of the situation and at what point do we continue to believe, in spite of evidence to the contrary, that some change in our behavior will impact some change in the other person's behavior?"

These are questions that demand wisdom and insight. The Light can lead us to understand our part in an abusive relationship, what attitudes we need to change, and what actions we need to take to resolve the situation.

In one case, a client had owed me money for many months. I soon discovered he had cheated twenty-three other people as well—all of us speakers at his conference. I felt some obligation to call it like it was and to see what could be done. I held this injustice up to the Light. Partly because of my input and the input of others, we banded together as a group. Finally, after about twenty emails and many attempts at phone calls, I wrote an email and said, "I never want to see your name again except on a check." Some months later, I did get a check with interest added. Perhaps there was some respect from him because I made such a strong statement. Eventually with persistence and some confrontation and much discussion within this group, most of us did get paid.

In retrospect, I feel I should have recognized the pattern much faster. I also feel that the team building brought those of us who were betrayed closer together. We helped each other, listened to each other, strategized together, and looked out for each other—trying to make sure all of us were treated fairly.

What Does the Light Do? It Can Be a Form of Intercessory Prayer

We usually think of prayer as dialogue. We communicate with God, and we usually use words to do that. Prayer is often vocalized. We tell God our concerns, our troubles, and our desires. Sometimes it's conversational—as if we're having a discussion with a dear friend. We might ask God for specific things, whether something to make our lives better or someone else's life better. We ask and sometimes plead for ourselves or someone else to be healed. Sometimes we even get angry with God and wonder why God isn't doing things the way we want them done. And we show our love for others by praying for them and being concerned for them.

Another aspect of prayer is meditative, or just "being" with God. This is a form of meditation that is practiced by Quakers in our worship services as well as on our own. It's a little like sitting with someone in silence and letting the Spirit do its work. We hold others and ourselves in the Light and envision them being embraced by that Warm Presence. Holding someone in the Light often means just sitting and imagining them being surrounded by Love. We tell them we are "Holding them in the Light" when we want to share in their joys and concerns. We hold them in the Light during sickness and crisis, as well as joys and sorrows. This kind of prayer is an effective way to increase our love, compassion, and care.

While we are holding someone in the Light, we might also ask, "What can I do to help?" The Light might move us into action—

something to show our love or concern—or the Light might simply comfort them because they know we care or because they feel something has changed. The Light may prompt us to bring food to them, write a note, bring flowers, visit them, or even create a unique gift. Holding them in the Light might simply comfort them. Quakers who are held in the Light often tell other Quakers "I could feel it" just as people who are prayed for say it made a big difference. There is a power in both of these forms of prayer, the vocal and the silent.

What Does the Light Do? It Can Illuminate Whether Something is a Temptation or a Blessing

In 1999, my husband and I began to voice our desire to move out of Los Angeles. We wondered if we could sustain our businesses if we moved. We both loved our work—Peter was a massage therapist and acupuncturist, and I was a script consultant, seminar leader, and author in the film industry—and we were concerned that a move could jeopardize our careers which had taken so many years to build.

We felt called to do what we were doing, and we felt our work had been blessed in many ways. But we also took seriously our increasing discomfort with living in a big city. We thought of various places to move to. I wanted to move to the Rocky Mountains in Colorado—a desire I'd had since I was thirteen and first entered the beautiful mountains. Peter wanted to move outside the United States, but I said there were no planes that went to a place called "outside the United States." After two years of discussion, he was still vague, and we both became open to moving to Colorado. We decided we would move within two to five years.

The day before 9/11, I had just finished giving a seminar in Denver. Just for fun, I decided to look at houses in the mountains near Colorado Springs. The first house I looked at was my dream house. But I told myself the timing was probably not quite right. The next day was 9/11. Since I couldn't fly home, I got into a rental car and headed straight home for Los Angeles.

As the weeks went on, I couldn't get this house out of my mind. I began to ponder whether this was a temptation which would ruin everything, or was it was a blessing that was right there in front of us and we just had to say "yes." After much contemplation, prayer, and discussion with fellow Quakers and with others, and turning over this big change in our minds, we both decided it was a blessing. We bought the house and moved in 2002. By reflecting on this, I realized that when we are blessed and say "yes" to the blessing, it leads us to happiness and fulfillment. We thank God almost daily and recognize that we were being led. The Light was illuminating a path that required a leap of faith—but it was a very good path to take. The desire that was planted inside me when I was thirteen was a true desire that was worth following.

What Does the Light Do? The Light Helps Us Discern Through a Clearness Committee

Quakers often use a process of discernment by calling together a group of three to five Friends to form a Clearness Committee.

Anybody who needs help seeking the Light for any issue they're confronting can call a Clearness Committee. They might be considering a move, a career change, resolution to a relationship conflict, or overcoming struggles they might be having as they enter a new stage in their life.

Quaker couples who want to be married with the blessing and care of the Meeting always call a Clearness Committees prior to the wedding. Individuals on this committee feel an obligation to make sure there is clarity about this step. Sometimes the committee suggests that the engaged couple wait before entering into marriage because they discover some impediment or some issue that needs to be ironed out before the couple moves forward. Most of the time, unity is reached and the wedding proceeds.

There's also always a Clearness Committee prior to a person joining a Friends Meeting. This helps ensure the clarity about the step of joining, and it's an opportunity for the person to share their spiritual journey and what is leading them to desire membership.

Quakers usually recommend people attend Meeting at least one year prior to joining in order to be knowledgeable about the faith and practice of Quakers. The Clearness Committee is not a time of judgment but of discernment.

Clearness Committees don't tell people what to do. It's a matter of helping them discern where the Light is leading them. This demands honesty and good listening skills from the committee. Often during this committee meeting, the group falls into silence to move deeper into their Center so they can help discern next steps. They may feel led to ask a question or to share an insight.

A Clearness Committee is a concept that can be used effectively by those who are not Quakers. They could call together a small group of wise people who they trust. They listen, discuss, and seek the Light. I have sometimes called together wise friends—some Quakers and some non-Quakers—to help me change my attitude towards a situation or person or to help give me courage to confront a problem.

What Does the Light Do? It Lights the Way

Many times, we go to friends and ask for advice and might even ask them what they would do in our situation. They bring their experiences to the table, discuss, and then go off and decide what to do and what advice to follow.

However, a Clearness Committee between friends/Friends is slightly different. If two people are discussing a situation and want to bring the Holy Spirit into this discussion, the time together might begin with silence, as well as positing a question that the friend is asking.

I have been part of several such one-on-one Clearness Committees. Once, a Friend wondered about changing fields or getting a different academic job. I felt my role in our discussion was to help discern where the Light was leading my friend.

My friend Nancy was teaching flute at a university, but there were many conflicts in her department, and she was not happy in this job. Her question was: "How do I find happiness, make a living, and still do what I love to do, which is teaching flute?" She thought of moving back to her hometown, living with her parents, and taking a break. She wondered about trying to get another job, and as she spoke, I discerned that her heart was not in teaching at a university. I was able to reflect back what I was hearing about her not being happy as a professor. There were certain things in her character, personality, and teaching approach that just didn't fit with the particular demands of teaching at a university where there was competitiveness and many judgments that didn't sit right with her.

Nancy then started talking to me about her private flute students, and she began to light up. She loved teaching these kids. I asked whether she could expand her teaching and how she might do that. I could see that there was doubt and fear, but I also saw how much she loved teaching private students which brought her great joy. Sometimes when we find clarity about our calling, the way unfolds. We follow the Light that comes from the Holy Spirit, and that allows the Holy Spirit to light the path further.

Nancy wondered if it would be financially viable to leave her academic job and focus just on her private students. It didn't take her long to build up her flute studio and leave her university job. She now has over twenty students, and for the last six or eight years she has lived within the Light and joy which clarified she had taken the right path. It was not a matter of advice, it was a matter of listening and feeding back to her where the Light began to shine.

What Does the Light Do? It's a Leading, Guiding Us Forward

These messages we receive are sometimes called Leadings. They might give us a new insight about an issue or problem. They might prod us to a new decision or action. They put a great responsibility upon the individual to take this leading seriously, to try to understand it, to sort through what it means for our lives and the lives of those around us. They help us discern whether we are to take immediate action or begin to prepare for future action. In many cases, these Leadings are discussed prayerfully with the whole Quaker community as the Quaker seeks further enlightenment. Many times, we look at our fears that might get in the way of following a leading, or understand the risk and upheaval it can make in our lives.

What Does the Light Do? It Can Lead Us to Social Action

Quakers believe that the Inward Light naturally leads us to outward action doing good in our neighborhoods, communities, and the world. There is no stopping place. This sometimes leads us to change our careers because we want to bring meaning into our lives but also to do good in the world. We find certain causes that speak to us, and we take a step forward to become involved. Some focus on issues dealing with the environment, equality and justice issues, or war and peace. There are currently many Meetings that feel called to address social issues such as immigration, climate change, Native rights, the Israeli-Palestinian continuing conflict, and with overcoming racial, sexist, and religious hatred and divisions.

What Does the Light Do? Sometimes It Seems to Disappear

In the Nativity story in the Bible, the three Magi, traveling to see the baby Jesus, lost sight of the star that guided them. They had been following it for some time, and then it seemed to disappear. Perhaps it was a cloudy night, or maybe they couldn't see it for some other reason. They stopped in Jerusalem to ask King Herod where the Messiah was to be born. The jealous king consulted his advisors and they said, "In Bethlehem." The Magi headed for Bethlehem, the star came out again, and showed them the way to the baby.

Sometimes the Light seems to have gone out, whether within ourselves or our neighborhood or our country or the entire planet.

I have seen and experienced the Light going out in situations that are dire and in situations that might not seem as important, but nevertheless impact us.

When I moved to Colorado in my 50s, I bought my first horse, Abby. This horse was beautiful, wonderful, and difficult. Things were not going well, and I returned to one of my previous riding teachers to see if she could analyze what was going on. She watched me in the arena and then unexpectedly walked out of the barn. I was hurt and confused. I followed her to understand why she would walk out on me. Tami, who was not a Quaker, described what she saw in Quaker terms: "Linda, the Light has gone out of both you and this horse, and I could not bear to watch it anymore. I beg you to come back and let me work with you and the horse. I will even do it for free because I can't stand to watch this happen." I came back to her and watched as day by day she helped my horse find her rhythm, and a discipline. Tami was firm but somehow always knew what the horse, and I, needed in order to progress. One of my greatest joys occurred on the day Tami told me to stand near the barn and just wait. She rode Abby down a hill until I lost sight of her. Suddenly, she came up the hill at a full gallop, which I had never seen the timid Abby do. Both of them looked like they were having the greatest time in their life. Soon she taught me to do the same on Abby. I found the Light and the joy, and Abby the horse did as well.

We have probably all watched the Light disappear from someone close to us and might have also gone through periods of time where the Light seemed to disappear within us. It is unbearable. And yet, the Light never goes out. It is a constant presence. This is a statement of faith and for most of us Quakers, it is a statement of our experience.

What Does the Light Do? It Asks Us to Follow It with Faith and Trust

Mary Linda McKinney describes her way of following the Light in an article titled "The Divine GPS" which was published in the *Friends Journal*:

> I'm given a Leading to do something. I have a sense that there

is a destination, but don't know where it is or what will happen when I get there. What I'm given is step one, which is like the first segment on a global positioning system. I see one tiny slice of an unknown larger trip, and all I have to do is faithfully get from where I am to the edge of the screen. Complete that, and I get to step two and three, and so on . . . The Divine GPS has a calm voice and never gets impatient . . . When I'm in a centered, open state, Spirit and I work well together . . . Trusting that resources will be available when I need them, and not stockpiling 'just in case' is an ongoing lesson. Sometimes . . . I'll get an idea of the destination to which I am headed and begin to think I know a better route . . . I forget to trust my divine GPS to guide me . . . When Spirit is guiding me though, I have to completely release attachment to understanding the purpose or the

> outcome, or learning about the impact I had.

Following inch by inch or step by step takes a tremendous amount of trust in the process. And yet, those of us who have trusted the star or trusted the divine GPS can be quite amazed that "following the Light we have" is enough. It is steady. It is often quite clear. And as we step forward in faith, the path unfolds ever more brightly.

Queries about Light

What words would you use to describe the Light Within?

Have you experienced the Light going out and then coming back to lead you?

Has the Light ever led you to life-changing decisions?

Chapter 2:
Sitting in Silence

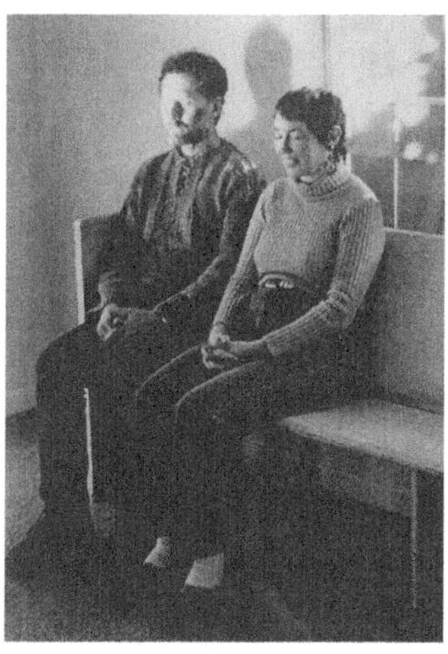

Linda Seger and husband Peter LeVar sitting in silence in Santa Monica Friends Meeting 1990s

Friends gather in silence, in a practice centuries old, to clear the way for the "still small voice." This silent gathering . . . is based on the belief that if one opens one's heart and listens, one can hear what is right, and can live out these inner teachings.. . . Silence refreshes the spirit and makes way for deep thinking about both ethical and intellectual quandaries.

American Friends Service Committee

True silence is the rest of the mind; and is to the spirit, what sleep is to the body, nourishment and refreshment.

WILLIAM PENN, QUAKER FOUNDER OF PENNSYLVANIA, 1682[4]

SILENCE IS ONE OF THE DEFINING QUALITIES of Quakers. We have Silent Meetings without ministers or leaders. There are no authorities to guide us or tell us what to do or how to think—no pastor, no prophet, no head of the church. The communication in many religious practices moves mainly to God, telling God what is wanted or needed. The person praying tells God how much they love Him, or what they are grateful for, or asks for mercy or blessings for themselves or for others. Quakers do that as well, but our focus is more on waiting for the Presence to speak to us out of the Silence.

Scripture refers to this as a "still small voice:"

> And, behold, the Lord passed by, and a great and strong wind rent the mountains, and brake in pieces the rocks before the Lord; but the Lord was not in the wind: and after the wind an earthquake; but the Lord was not in the earthquake: and after the earthquake a fire; but the Lord was not in the fire: and after the fire a still small voice.
>
> ~1 Kings 19:11–12 (KJV)

How Do We Worship?

Our Quaker worship practice is quite simple. We sit in a circle. Usually bow our heads. Get Still. And to the outsider, we just seem to sit there. And yet, there is a sense that something is happening. If it weren't, why would we continue?

For non-Quakers who enter a Meeting, this takes some getting used to.

Many people are afraid of silence. Some don't know what to do with it. Some find it odd. Our society seems to love noise. Many people have radios and televisions playing in the background in their homes. It's not unusual to go to some worship services in Protestant or Catholic churches and hear a buzz as people greet each other, catch up on each other's news of the week, and share their excitement about seeing each other.

Quakers embrace Silence and find the emptiness of sacred space to be quite filled, not with thoughts as much as with light and expectant waiting. It is a different kind of approach, but one that can be integrated into anyone's spiritual life.

What Does Silence Do?

A good, rich Silence, at the very least, quiets the mind. This is the basis of meditation in all practices from Buddhists to Catholics to Self-Realization Fellowship to anybody who meditates.

I used to think that I was supposed to have something going on in my mind all the time. And I was quite good at doing that. But all those thoughts and churnings and irritations and jumblings tend to dart all over the place and it's often difficult to get a handle on what is at the Center. We can't quite reach deep enough or go far enough into our minds to find stillness and peace. We want to quell the chaos and we have trouble figuring out how to do that. Yet something draws us in to believe that good things will come if we could only learn to be comfortable in this quiet place.

The Undistracted Stillness of the Quiet River

Many of us come to Quakerism from other practices of meditation. My husband, Peter, learned Transcendental Meditation in the 1970s and finds it helps him to move into the Quiet. There are Quakers who practice Buddhist meditation. Carlton Gamer, who was one of the founders of the Colorado Springs Friends Meeting, was both a Buddhist and a Quaker. Part of his practice included "Putting distracting thoughts under little logs that move past, down the river, and out of sight so I can move back into the stillness."

He described the difference between the Buddhist Silence and the Quaker Silence:

"The Buddhist goal is to forget the self and lose the self. Even though meditation, in itself, is goalless, part of the goal is enlightenment so the self or the ego drops away. This result brings illumination, clarity, wisdom, and peace."

Carlton says the Quaker goal is "to create a heightened awareness of what's going on around me and awareness of the self in relationship to others and in relationship to the larger world."

Ann Grant Martin from the same Meeting, who also has a Buddhist practice, says:

> Both meditations include stopping engagement in all activities. Both Quakers and Buddhists focus on listening during their time of prayer or meditation. However, the source of information that may be realized is different. Many Quakers believe that God is the source of the message they receive, whereas Buddhists do not. Quakers gain the message from outside them. Buddhists realize an insight from

> inside themselves. My experience has been that the Buddhist insight or Quaker message was in me all along, I just had to get quiet enough to hear it.

Dennis Redfield from Portland, Maine, is also both a Buddhist and a Quaker. He says:

> Meditation is a scary word. I've been advised to avoid it when referring to what happens in Meeting for Worship. I find the term "sitting" to be most appropriate. My Buddhist friends usually refer to what we do 'on the cushion' as sitting. Likewise, I sit with my Quaker Friends during Meeting for worship. Be still, and know. I don't draw a strong line between silent sitting as a Buddhist and Silent Worship as a Quaker. The friends I sit with in each group change, the spiritual practice does not. We make space for our souls to be touched by God.

We seek a closer relationship with that mysterious Presence which is both higher and deeper than we are, even in seeking. Somehow that Presence finds us—at least at times. Something happens that begins to move us, touch us, and transform us. This doesn't mean it's easy.

Dwelling in the Silence, for most of us, is a learning experience over a long period of time. Cathleen, from Santa Monica says, "I feel that I'm inept at moving into silent worship. My strength is that I keep showing up." And she has for over fifty years.

Showing up begins to change us, in our ability to be silent in worship and in our ability to live our lives with a reflective silence that we can draw upon daily.

How Do We Do This?

Quaker Silent Worship often means that Quakers have to find their own way, because there is no training.

Ann from Colorado Springs explains:

> There is scant information or instruction about how to spend an hour in Silence. Buddhists, on the

other hand, offer copious amounts of education about meditation. They write books, make movies, teach classes, and give talks about how to meditate. They advise a beginner to begin with only five minutes of meditation instead of an hour as in a Quaker meeting for worship. Since there is no expectation of communicating with a "higher power" during a Buddhist meditation period, focusing on the breath is encouraged. Buddhist meditation can be a time of emptying the mind and also a time of observing how busy the mind is. It all counts. The result of a regular meditation practice for me and others is having a calm, happy demeanor. Someone once said to me, "I want some of your peace."

In Quakerism, We are Seeking the Light within Ourselves and within Others

Silence opens up the way for us to seek the Light. Dennis says, "As my practice grew, I was reminded by older and wiser Quakers, that if I could not see the light within my neighbors, that I should look first to the darkness in my own heart, to see what was clouding my vision."

Cathleen from Santa Monica clarifies this takes time:

> Little by little, sometimes over a period of years, Truth gathers itself together and strikes root. Then life changes. The great comfort of being in a Friends Meeting is to feel the presence of those whom you know. We all struggle with life's challenges. We're all in this together. We feel for one another and in forgiving, accepting, and supporting each other, we experience God's love.
>
> My method of centering is to hold those I love in the Light.

> When my mind wanders, I let it. Fighting these thoughts just makes them stronger. But often I wonder what makes these thoughts important. What lies behind them? Are they a distraction from some important spiritual message or is the important spiritual message contained in the thought?

Stan Searl from Santa Monica Friends Meeting examined how different Quakers understand Silence. In his book, *The Meanings of Silence in Quaker Worship*, some of these Friends have a process similar to Cathleen's.

A Friend from Buffalo, New York, says:

> People have somehow characterized it as to blank their mind, clear their mind. My experience is not like that . . . My experience is letting all the stuff come forward. For me, it's letting the items of stress or discomfort or anger, periods of anger, scenes of anger come forward, and I've characterized

this, visualized this, as somehow like an attic room, only an attic room with myself in the middle and allowing the trap door to open . . . And so I have felt that we are centering down . . . I feel as if it's a process of disconnecting and becoming emancipated from it and getting connected with things in myself and with other people.

We are trying to get out of the busyness that is such a part of our lives so another voice can emerge. We are trying to settle down and disentangle. We are trying to quiet the churnings and the irritations. Sometimes in that settling down we sense a problem or an issue for a period of time—sometimes a day, a month, or a season. It's a little bit like simmering on a very low heat so that our natural, heated up side is turned down. We are lowering the temperature so we don't boil over. Gradually we then cool off. This allows us to see more clearly.[5]

Cathleen continues:

> So yes, I do ponder. But more importantly, I hold up my problems to God if only because they seem beyond my ability to understand or repair. I trust in a higher wisdom. I rest in the Arms. I see this gathering of knowledge like gathering smoke. It takes me a long time to assemble a form. But this is sacred smoke. Meaning reveals itself to the faithful.

Like Cathleen, many of us find it difficult to move into this Silence. We have different techniques for doing this. My husband often begins by saying the Lord's Prayer and praying for people he knows until the Silence embraces and envelopes him. I often begin by reading a page of Quaker writings or some Bible verses. Some use other scripture such as the Twenty-third Psalm or perhaps the quote from Samuel in the Hebrew scriptures, "Speak; Lord; for thy servant heareth" (1 Samuel 3:9–10 KJV).

A Catholic nun recommended that when I have problems getting into the Quiet, that I simply state my intention to God: "God, I intend to be present to you in this time of worship."

When I'm struggling with something, I sometimes do a meditation I learned which is designed to quiet my mind. I imagine going down an elevator, floor by floor, into a deeper space. By counting the floors, my mind gets quieter, until I reach the bottom floor, wherever that may be. One day when I was doing this meditation, I decided to continue the visualization by walking out of the elevator to see where I was. I found myself in a small railroad depot. I looked across the road and saw a very low adobe wall and a big adobe arch. I crossed the street, wondering who I would see beyond that low wall. I walked into a garden and saw a Jesus figure—not in biblical robes, but in a lumberjack shirt and jeans. We sat on the wall together and I told him what was irritating me. And of course, I got good advice. Sometimes, when I do this meditation, Jesus and I walk toward a fountain where is a beautiful, very big shining ray of light and we simply stand in that light, which gives me a tremendous sense of calm.

In the best of my meditation times, I begin by imagining a ray of light, and I stand just outside of it looking up at it, and allowing it to invite me in. As I stand inside of it, my mind becomes clear and empty, and I sometimes define it as "basking in the Presence of God." I don't get there very often. But when I do, it is truly a sacred space.

Maggie from Portland, Maine, uses a classic meditation:

> My process is connected with my love for the Maine Coast. I begin with imagining visually the smallest rock that I associate with the coast. The rocks are smooth and small and beautiful colors. I look at that rock to begin the process of meditating. The next rock is a little bit bigger, not smooth but with crags and fissures. Each time

> the rocks get bigger and bigger until I reach the boulder that sits right on the water. I can sit on the boulder and silence takes over. When I become distracted, I return to the stones. The quality of silence is a combination of blankness and light. I know when I have received a message I need to share, I start to shake and the Light gets stronger. There is a sense of fear.

That fear often leads us to speak aloud in Meeting. We got our name, Quakers, because we shook and had such fervor when we spoke to the group.

Stan Searle asked an older Quaker woman who lived near Saratoga Springs in Upstate New York how she got started in worship.[6]

She started to talk about the silence and "paused and closed her eyes."

> "Ever do the dead man's float?" she asked.
>
> Stan said, "Oh Sure."

> "All right. That's what it's like. You just 'rest' in the silence. There is a poem of John Greenleaf Whittier's called 'The 'The Meeting.'"[7]

> She quoted a few lines from memory: "And from the silence multiplied/By these still forms on either side,/The world that time and sense have known/Falls off and leaves us alone." That's it.

The Quiet often brings us solutions to a problem, insights, personal revelations, or simply an ability to quiet the struggle and the chaos. Diana from Portland, Maine, says:

> Sometimes I start with a statement or question as a prompt to my spirit to focus. I don't try to solve the problem. I trust that the openness and quiet will bring me the answer.

We learn to trust that the Spirit is present in that quiet Center. This doesn't mean that everything we hear when we are in that space is taken as Gospel Truth. We still have to discern. We have to test the waters. We take the plumb line and we test it against various verses and ideas in the Bible, perhaps what other Quakers have written, and we might even discuss with others what we believe we heard. We are not necessarily perfect receivers, and we don't take for granted that we are the Great Instrument of God. We may or may not be. We try to put pride and ego aside and if necessary, keep listening.

Listening to the Nudges

Out of this silence, at times, comes a nudge to do something. We presume these nudges come from the Holy Spirit, because in that sacred silence, there is love and unity. If we're conflicted, we're not in that space yet, although we might be working at centering ourselves to get deep enough to hear these proddings and messages.

The nudges come in different forms. Sometimes they're an idea that keeps pushing at us, letting us know it's time for a change. Sometimes it's an emotion that we might otherwise easily dismiss but that might be important. That irritant or the churning of the stomach or the moment of anger and discontent might actually be coming from the Holy Spirit in order to push us to wake up, pay attention—letting us know that something is wrong and needs to be addressed.

I have experienced those irritations at times when I am in a relationship with someone who is toxic. My natural inclination was to tell myself "Be nice!" And that was my problem. Sitting in the Silence helped take away the irritation behind it and helped me see clearly that this person was not good for me, and I needed to kindly disengage without hard feelings.

The nudge might be telling us to change our lives and allow ourselves to be transformed. It might nudge us to change our career, or marry the terrific person we're dating, or move to a new location. It might be a nudge that says, "It's okay to leave everything behind and go to this new life. You'll be safe. You can trust it. There will be good people there." We might then begin to feel calm and all the junk that's been swirling around seems to move aside so we can see the path clearly. Perhaps fear was getting in the way of making a decision. The Light in the forest revealed the way to go.

I have learned to take the smallest nudges seriously. The Holy Spirit not only cares about world-changing events, but also cares about the tiniest moments of kindness and compassion. Some time ago, my friend Rose had COVID, and when I asked what we could do for her and her husband, Bob, she couldn't think of anything. She said they didn't need food and they were hunkering down. She added that they were quite ill and weren't really thinking straight. I sat in our Silent Meeting, and suddenly had the idea of dropping off two yellow roses. I knew that yellow roses meant family and friendship and had once told her about this meaning. I left two yellow roses by her back door and let her know they were there.

The test of whether this nudge came from the Holy Spirit is partly by the response to the action. Obviously if she had told me she hated roses, I would have to re-think that nudge. But she loved the roses. Rose told me, "The roses lasted for two weeks. I took them from room to room and they filled each room with a beautiful fragrance."

These little pushes lead to good things if they come from the Holy Spirit. If they lead to dissension and conflict and mean-spiritedness or anger, there is something wrong either with the nudge itself or our interpretation of it. Not every nudge is coming from a Holy Place. I sometimes have to ask, "Is this nudge a temptation or a blessing?"

Sometimes the Silence helps us find our integrity in a situation. What is the right path? Is our self-righteousness getting in the way of doing the right thing? Are we so sure that we are right that we cling to a pre-made decision and we just want God to agree? Are we open enough to let a better choice emerge?

Sometimes the Silence simply gives us the space to sit down, season a decision, ponder, think about it in new ways, and let things simmer.

Silence can take away the friction between us and others. Someone irritates us, and we hold them in our mind in that Silence and see them in a new light. They too are struggling. Maybe they're making some awful decisions that are causing lots of problems for a lot of people, but we gain the strength and the goodwill that allows us to pray for them and love them in spite of their imperfections and our own.

Seeking the Quiet Place

In 1966, when I was in college, I wrote a poem which I re-discovered recently when going through old boxes of memorabilia. I was not a Quaker until 1970, but I was surprised how this poem clarified my desire for that quiet place within me:

> Little, bustling woman
> why do you flit-flit about?
> needle pin thread
> need time to taste yesterday's work
> grandmother rocker
> needs time to smell the sunlight
> the not-quite-young mind of little,
> bustling woman

needs time to see.
Flitting is for sparrows
who live in sunlight
who are sunlight—
not for little bustling minds
For whom sunlight was made.

Part of our process is to move into that Silent space that is filled with a sacred emptiness. It is a lovely quiet where a sense of time ceases.

Nudges Can Lead Us to Social Justice

What I want in life is peace and joy. Others might want love and safety. Trust. A little more compassion to and from others. Fewer obstacles that get in the way of a better life. We can get worn down and exhausted just from the process of living and dealing with life's difficulties.

The movement of the Spirit within us leads to the movement of the Spirit outside of us and into the world. It is a natural movement. As within, so without. Our work for a better world comes out of the silence that we practice.

Quakers are known worldwide for our commitment to social justice. We were some of the first abolitionists. We were at the forefront of the women's movement in the 1840s. We were in the foreground of prison reform. We are known for our peace efforts. These include working with refugees and migrants and the poor and the homeless and the oppressed—just as the Bible asks us to do.

It isn't just about making our own personal lives better. We keep feeling the movement outward to kind acts in our neighborhoods, in our cities, in our countries, and in our world. The Holy Spirit has no boundaries.

What Happens in the Stillness?

The Light, God, the Source, the Living Waters—whatever you might call that Goodness and Truth that resides at the Center—leads us and guides us, helps us figure things out and reconfigure, gives us a bigger way of looking at life, and helps us find what is needed. This gives us clarity to gain a new perspective or to take different action. Quakers try to take all those nudges seriously—both big and small.

Silence allows us to go beyond words and sink deeply below the clutter and then to move outward. Beth Bussiere from Portland (Maine) Friends Meeting describes it as:

> Down to the Silence
>
> Down to the Living Waters
>
> Down to the Source that connects us all.

Queries about Silence

How difficult is it for me to move into the Silence?

What methods and rituals do I use to help me settle into the Silence?

How do I return to Silence and overcome the distractions and the frenetic thoughts that keep me from centering down?

The SPICES

Simplicity

Peace

Integrity

Community

Equality

Stewardship

The testimonies bear witness to the truth, as Friends in community perceive it—truth known through relationship with God. They do not exist in any rigid, written form; nor are they imposed in any way. Quakers search for how the testimonies can best be expressed in their own lives. Quaker testimonies are expressions of the commitment to put beliefs into practice. While attempting to live in concert with these teachings, Quakers are tender with themselves and with each other when they fall short, ready to recommit and try again.

THE AMERICAN FRIENDS SERVICE COMMITTEE

Quakers try to allow the Light to guide them as they come to terms with what it means to be a Quaker, and to follow these testimonies: Simplicity, Peace, Integrity, Community, Equality, Stewardship. They are called The SPICES to help us remember them.

Instead of dogmas and creeds, Quakers have testimonies which guide us, challenge us, and lead us. These testimonies do not exist in any rigid, written form; nor are they imposed in any way. They witness to what our experience is and what we are called to do. It is part of our Faith and Practice.

Quakers are encouraged to search for how the testimonies can best be expressed in their family lives, their careers, the conflicts they encounter, and the ever-rippling effect of their decisions and actions as they apply them to all relationships locally and internationally. They ponder these, reflect on these, and think about how they relate to their own situations. They test them with the Spirit and try to evolve and transform their spiritual lives.

Sara Primo, who is the head of Friends School of Portland, an independent Quaker day school for grades preschool–8 in Portland, Maine, says:

> SPICES are taught specifically in our school. We talk about the testimonies and practice them. Students have projects about them. The Stewardship Testimony leads them to various actions that care for the environment. The Peace Testimony leads them into new ways of dealing with others when they disagree. They develop a consciousness about social justice, racism and moral development. Integrity of course is the core of so much including honesty, being explicit, tending to each other and having direct communication. Simplicity helps us to understand what is distracting us. We bring our Community together for worship, integrating all the grades. We teach the children that when the Community is disrupted, there

> needs to be reflection and repair. And we help the students reflect on what they have done when their behavior needs to be addressed. And how it has potentially hurt or affected others.

Some Quakers have problems with the idea of testimonies and don't find them helpful because they can seem too much like a creed. They can seem limiting. We always want to remember that it is the Inward Light, which is our Source.

To others of us, certainly me included, they guide us and challenge us. Personally, I find these words rich with meaning since they help me clarify parts of my life that might not align with my faith and values.

The Simplicity Testimony has been particularly challenging to me because I had a career in the film industry that included national and international travel, working with many different types of people, complex professional and personal relationships, and the chaos and anxiety and competitiveness that can come when working in an industry that is often ego driven and unfair. I had to ask myself, "How do I achieve Simplicity in a complex context?"

The Peace Testimony has been very challenging for many Quakers and non-Quakers because it doesn't seem to make sense in a violent world. The Peace Testimony is about more than being anti-war. For me, it has helped me to be calm in the midst of crises and chaotic situations, and it taught me to respect my adversaries and find ways to resolve conflict.

Integrity has always been important to me, even as a small child. This was one of the easiest testimonies for me because I was taught to be honest, and yet this testimony helped me realize I wasn't always telling the truth. After I became a Quaker, this testimony continued to rub at me in those times when I was not honest.

The Community Testimony led me to do more research and more thinking over the years about what community actually meant. This recently included attending a five-evening course via Zoom about Quaker Community and the challenges we face. We are often small Meetings and there are times there are disagreements and irritations and conflicts. I began to value the importance of community and to make it my intention to be part of healthy communities and to work to keep them healthy.

The Equality Testimony has been the guide in my life as a career woman in the film business as well as a woman who went to seminary when only ten percent of my class were women. This testimony strengthened me to stand up for my equal right to study theology as well as to create a career that would be equally paid and equally respected as any man's career.

The Stewardship Testimony has been a more current challenge. It is the newest testimony and was added as Quakers began to be more aware of the social justice aspects of climate change as well as our responsibility to create a better world. Applying this testimony to my own life is an ongoing process. I am thinking more about how to apply this testimony in my own personal life while continuing my social concerns for a more sustainable and just culture.

In spite of some conflict around testimonies, I find it fascinating to hear how other Quakers apply these testimonies in their own lives.

The rest of this book will be examining how these testimonies can be deepened within Quakers and integrated into the spiritual life of any spiritual person. It is through the Light that they come to terms with this and other testimonies in one way or another.

PART 2:
The Testimonies

Chapter 3:
The Simplicity Testimony

Chestnut Hill Friends Meeting House, Philadelphia PA[8]

Friends believe in simple living . . . In contemporary terms, Friends try to live lives in which activities and possessions do not get in the way. . . . to hear the 'still small voice' within. . . . In our personal lives, simplicity may mean limiting our consumerism—and resisting over-commitment, so that we have time to care for ourselves and to be present with one another.

American Friends Service Committee

I live my life to be free of cumber.

JOHN WOOLMAN (1720–1772)

MANY OF US YEARN FOR A SIMPLER LIFE. We find there are too many distractions that surround us. The honking horns, the phone calls that interrupt us, the clutter that piles up in our homes, and the blaring television beckons to us. Our lives are filled with frenetic energy—going to and from appointments, social engagements, committees, the push and pull from children and spouses and friends.

Social media demands that we are "in the know" about important current events. We want others to know of our comings and goings, so we take photos and write texts. If we have careers, we have to keep up with our colleagues, with marketing, with seeing and being seen by the people who can help move us forward.

For some Quakers, this is not a temptation and they deliberately choose careers that don't have these demands. Other Quakers move into a busy life and search for a way to keep their Center despite the rush around them. There are some Quakers who question whether Simplicity should be one of our testimonies. It seems to some that this is either covered by the other testimonies in one way or another, or that it doesn't have the weight of the Peace, Integrity, Community, Equality, and Stewardship Testimonies.

But Simplicity is the inward beginning of what becomes the outward work. Historically, it has been a key part of Quakerism.

Early Quakers wore plain clothes dress, much like the Amish and Mennonites. If you've seen pictures of Amish or Quaker women, they are usually shown in a gray or black long skirt, a white blouse with no frills or flounces. No decorations, no jewelry. Color and jewels and ornamentation were considered vain and called attention to one's self. Quaker men wore black suits and a hat they refused to doff to anyone because everyone was considered equal.

Quakers, from their very beginnings in the 1600s, saw Simplicity as an important part of the spiritual life. They recognized that it is difficult to listen to the Holy Spirit if our lives are burdened with activities and possessions and if the load is heavy. They understood that the perceived need by our society and culture to achieve a certain standard of wealth, power, and reputation can get in the way of listening to the Holy Spirit.

They rejected the social and cultural push of status and wealth. The Testimony of Simplicity guided them to lead lives of authenticity that put the focus on the inner life rather than what they saw as outer entrapments.

Simplicity in the Meeting House

Simplicity in Quakerism might best be seen in Quaker Meeting houses. They are designed to have few distractions. There is no stained glass, no embroidered cushions, no pictures or banners or hangings on the wall, no altars or pulpits. Just wooden pews, simple chairs, and plain windows to let in the light.

The Meeting house provides a place that makes it easier for us to center into that quiet, still, sacred place where we can be in touch with our Center. Most people close their eyes during worship so there is no need for art that pulls our attention.

Most Meeting houses have chairs in a circle. Rarely is there anything in the middle of the circle, although some Meeting Houses have a small table with a candle, perhaps a few flowers, sometimes even a Bible.

It's not just the lack of art that defines a Quaker Meeting house. Light comes through windows and softly plays on surfaces. It is both a metaphor of the Light Within and it is also a physical expression of the beauty of light that brings clarity and purity and, metaphorically, sheds light on issues and ponderings.

This same simplicity extends to materials used in a Quaker Meeting house. Generally, the pews are wood, often from trees that grow in the surrounding area. Other natural materials from the locality are often used—such as brick or stone that is locally quarried.

The Quaker aesthetic, with its simple lines, has a similarity to the aesthetics of the Shakers and the Amish, known for their beautiful woodworking.

How Do We Keep Our Living Spaces Simple?

Just as the Meeting houses are designed to help us center and nurture our ability to connect with the Holy Spirit, our living spaces have the same potential.

Sometimes the word 'balance' or 'harmony' is used to describe this kind of simplicity.

Lyn Ballou from Portland, Maine, says:

> I think my word for lifestyle simplicity would be 'moderation.' There can be an air about advocating for what I would call extreme plainness in daily life that harks back to the teaching of Jesus who

> asks us to give up everything and follow Him. I think most Quakers have figured out over our three centuries of existence that it is not possible for most people to create a family and live with some security under those circumstances. So, we do live in comfort, appreciate beauty and those who create it, and try to share any overabundance.

Cathleen from Santa Monica says:

> If you simplify your possessions, you have what you need and you aren't burdened with a larger and larger financial 'nut.' I give away anything I haven't used in a year or two. My only addiction is CDs and books. I have lots of music and books, many of which I haven't listened to or read for at least three to ten years. Sometimes I refer to them as my Horcrux a la the *Harry Potter* series. It's as if some part of my soul will depart unless these are in the house. It's obviously a form of idolatry.

Are Art and Simplicity Mutually Exclusive?

Those of us who are in the arts sometimes feel a conflict between the plainness that is part of the Quaker aesthetics and our love for beauty that fulfills us. What nurtures us is very different from person to person. What some might call over-decorating, others call warm and cozy.

Lyn from Portland, Maine, says:

> Our recently departed member Arthur Fink was always very fired up about that, as he believed art and beauty were all part of spirituality—'Spirit-led,' he would have said. I do not think simplicity always means plainness. It does as to one's house of worship—early Quakers were certainly reacting to the distractions of stained glass, incense, icons, statues, and ornate furniture for the clergy. They wanted to concentrate on their inner and outer direct relationship with God so they simplified their

> worship spaces. I think we still feel that way about our Meeting Houses.

Aesthetics have been a form of spirituality in many other traditions. The Japanese aesthetic usually has one beautiful art object or a flower arrangement that helps them focus their meditation. This leads to a sense of tranquility in their surroundings, which can include a garden, a window that lets in the light and shows the view, and even the beautifully decorated teacups and teapot used in a Japanese tea ceremony.

What we have in our homes shows our values and what we need to feed our souls, just as our experience with the Spirit leads us into different careers and decisions.

Why Is the Simple Life Important?

Leonard Kenworthy, a Quaker Aid Worker says, “Living simply is the right ordering of our lives and priorities.”

Most Quakers are fully engaged in the complexities of modern life. They are lawyers and consultants, teachers and social workers, actors and artists. Their challenge is different than those religious groups that withdraw from the world in order to live simply, such as the Amish, some Mennonite groups, and Catholic nuns or monks who withdraw to convents and monasteries. Quakers are fully in the world and working to make a better world with all the variety that we might see from many other groups.

Like most people who engage in this world, our busy lives are demanding. Our thoughts roam. We start to do one thing and get interrupted and then can't remember what we were going to do. Ideas run through our minds, leading to actions that overwhelm us. There are kids to take to soccer and baseball games, gymnastics and dance lessons, doctor and dentist appointments. There is the cooking to be done three times a day. It's easy to get overwhelmed and to simply not have time for things of the Spirit. How do Quakers find simplicity in these complex lives?

Quakerism emphasizes Centering and settling down and taking time to calm our inner life so that what flows out of us in terms of actions and behavior has a natural rhythm that determines how we live our outward lives.

Quakerism might be one of the few religious practices that teach us to say "no" to overly committing our time. In most churches, we're asked to serve on committees, to provide hospitality, to visit the sick, and to bring food for the potluck on Sunday. Quakerism asks us to take a moment before saying "yes" to a request that demands our time and skills. We ask ourselves if this request is in line with what we are called to do by the Spirit and whether this will overextend us so that we end up being frenetic and frustrated.

We try to balance that inner need with our sense of responsibility to social justice and to responding to those in need. It is a delicate balance between the inner and outer life, because the flow between the two of them needs to remain in harmony.

John Woolman approached this problem in a way that Quakers often do. He was a tailor in the 1700s. He discovered that the demand for his services was getting in the way of his spiritual practice. He pulled back from his work, transitioning to part time, so that he had more time to do spiritual work. He wanted to live his life "free of cumber."

We might approach this need for more time to center by deciding not to answer our phones every time they ring and letting our answering machine do the work for us at certain times of the day. Sometimes it means texting instead of calling and at the same time, resisting the temptation to look at emails or texts every time we receive a notification.

In my case, as an author and script consultant and seminar leader, I tried to take moments of silence and a few deep breaths as I moved from one activity to the next, preparing myself for a new rhythm. I would do administrative work, sit for a few minutes, work on a report, sit, practice piano, sit, cook, sit—brief moments of silence allow us to center from one activity to the next.

One of my fellow author friends once jokingly said, "If I haven't written two books before breakfast, I don't feel like I've accomplished anything." I could relate to that, but it's a temptation to be resisted.

Bringing Meditation Practices into Our Lives

It's easy to fall into a pattern where we think of our spiritual life as something we do at certain times, and then we do our activity. It's as if the breathing or the rituals or the silence or the centering that we do prepares us to do the next activity with more calm and tranquility.

But every activity in our lives has the potential to bring us in touch with the Spirit while doing the activity. Some of the great Catholic saints did work like cooking and cleaning as a meditation. St. Theresa of Avila says, "God is in the pots and pans."

Brother Lawrence was called "The Kitchen Saint" because he was a cook. He says:

> The time of business does not differ with me from the time of prayer; and in the noise and clatter of my kitchen, . . . I possess God in as great tranquility as if I were on my knees. . . . I turn my little omelet in the pan for the love of God.

Chopping vegetables has a calming rhythm to it. The rhythm of the knife and the chopping board can be a meditation. Cleaning house, playing piano, weeding the roses, and taking a walk can all be done with calm and tranquility. If we but notice and breathe down into our depths, all of our activities can be addressed with a calm spirit.

Feel the Rhythm

One of my favorite quotes comes from the Australian film, *Strictly Ballroom*, about two ballroom dancers trying to win a competition. They are doing the steps correctly but something is missing. The grandmother asks the dancers, "Where do you feel the rhythm?" The dancers start to move their feet. Grandma says, "No, no." She puts her hand on the boy's heart and says, "Here. Feel the rhythm. Don't be afraid."

How do we create a rhythm in our life where our daily movements allow room for spiritual calm? How do we do the work of our professional and personal lives while allowing room to listen to the Holy Spirit?

One of my non-Quaker friends was a role model for me. Dulcie Smart produces the evening news for a major television station in Berlin, Germany. She told me, "This is a high-stress job and the timing has to be exact. I found I was doing my job totally on adrenaline, and I realized I would burn myself out very quickly. I loved the job, and I didn't want to quit, but I had to find a way to do this in a more centered way. I began to set up my life so every day I did yoga for half an hour. My work hours were very strange, from 4 p.m. to midnight. So, I always gave myself time to center when I got home, then would get a good night's sleep and do yoga first thing in the morning. I also tried to eliminate distractions so things in my life were calm and I could take that calm into my work."

When I stayed with Dulcie for a few days on several different occasions, she was very clear about her schedule so I knew not to interrupt her during those times, and I understood how important her rituals were to her.

Like Dulcie, I want my life to flow from the time I get up in the morning to the time I go to sleep in the evening. The actions that we take, if they are done with a sense of kindness and integrity, are worthy and valuable. There is an intrinsic rhythm to these activities, and when we find that rhythm, we don't feel rushed and instead feel focused and calm. The Spirit is in the task itself, and often leads us to find joy in the details. Sometimes this is called Flow—getting into the flow of that task, which often means we slow down our breathing, relax into what we are doing, and feel calm while we are doing it—even if it's something that seems on the surface to be fast-paced. Runners use rhythmic breathing techniques to slow down their breathing, make them more efficient, and help them relax into the run.

Sometimes deliberately slowing down the work also helps us become more efficient, because we are not becoming frenetic and not seeing our work as just a To Do list.

De-Cluttering

Just as there is clutter inside of our lives, there is plenty of clutter outside. Papers pile up. Books don't get put back in the bookcase. Mail sits for days on the kitchen table. Toys—whether for children or cats or dogs—trip us as we move from activity to activity.

Some people hire professional organizers to make their closets and their rooms calmer and less frustrating. Others watch YouTube to learn how to "Feng Shui" their spaces.

Cathleen from Santa Monica says,

> I've begun to store pots and pans in the cupboards just to clear the clutter. The kitchen is so much

> calmer. Maybe like the pots and pans, I could do more clearing away in other areas of my house and only keep out that which I am working on at the moment. I like the saying 'a place for everything and everything in its place.' Sometimes this demands a bit of meditation to figure out what that place is.

Sometimes there isn't a place for all the things in our homes and it's time to start giving things away. How do we decide when something nurtures us and when it burdens us?

Cathleen continues:

> I've seen programs on TV, like *Sparking Joy* with Marie Kondo, who tell us to keep only those things that "spark joy."
>
> We can look at the obstacles and frustrations in our daily life and ponder what can be removed. We might ask ourselves, "Why am I constantly walking across the room to get a fork or knife? Why are

> my knives never near the cutting board? Why are the pots and pans never near the stove? Why am I always tripping over the rug? Why can't I find my winter coat?

Avoiding the frustrations that often run our lives is part of creating the simple life. Although thinking about these frustrations might seem trivial, they are another way to make our lives more centered. We want to be in the eye of the storm, not the storm.

It's Not About Excess: Less Is More

Quakers also see Simplicity as part of a social justice issue. Consumerism can drive us and have negative effects on our entire society.

Adopting plain dress removed the need of the Quakers to become consumers who changed clothes with every change of style, which meant buying something, wearing it a few times, and either throwing it away or donating it to a thrift store. Consumerism uses up natural resources, sometimes raping the environment, and sometimes using child labor or workers who are not paid a fair wage. Excess leads to the pile-up of waste in our landfills. It can lead to putting our money into goods that are not of service to the workers or the consumers.

Consumerism can create a push to live beyond our income. It creates a barrier between the rich and the poor, the haves and the have nots. We obsess over material things and avert our eyes from the things of the Spirit. Our desire to have more and more and to compete and keep up with others makes us frantic about our lives rather than serene.

In our society, many people are addicted to online shopping. The rush comes from researching an item, finding it on sale, clicking "Buy Now," anticipating its arrival, and the excitement when the package appears on the doorstep. People may not ever use the item or even open the package. But if something isn't being delivered every week, they grow anxious.

Scarcity thinking recognizes that if there is barrenness within, we are compelled to fill it with stuff in our outer lives. Buying things is a comfort. Consumerism comes from the fear of not having enough or being enough or the fear of missing out. We justify our purchase even though it cuts into our finances and puts ourselves at risk. A sale can govern our lives and make us believe that we better get it now or we will definitely lose out. We are often unable to distinguish between our wants and our needs. When we do buy something that we believe we need, we sometimes later find out we didn't make a wise purchase.

Quaker John Woolman had a different idea about clothes and consumerism. He believed in investing in one high-quality suit. He wanted clothes that would last for years so he would not need to spend his time thinking about what to wear and not have to continually replace clothes.

When I started giving seminars on screenwriting in the mid-1980s, I pondered what John Woolman's concept would mean for me as a Quaker woman in the

Hollywood film industry. I found this idea quite profound. I decided to have a high-quality blouse made that was colorful and professional. That was my Day 1 seminar outfit. Then I bought a high-quality Day 2 outfit. Since I did two-day seminars and moved from country to country, it didn't matter if I wore the same clothes. Over the years I made some small repairs and subtle changes. It's now been more than thirty-five years, and I am still wearing these clothes and they are still beautiful.

There is a saying, "What you have is enough." There is another saying, "They are rich who are content with what they have." We don't always need more and more, we need to know what we need and look for quality, not quantity.

Keeping Our Spiritual Power

If we think of the Holy Spirit as guiding us to create more authentic lives, this form of inner authenticity will be expressed differently in an outward fashion. A Quaker corporate executive will express simplicity differently than a person who works at home wearing comfortable clothes or pj's. A person whose work demands a heavy travel schedule will find different ways to simplify their time in airplanes and hotels.

Quakers make these decisions based on personal experience combined with an understanding of Quaker history. We seek the Light to guide us and believe that the Light is always available, even for things that might seem unimportant. We don't have a rule book that tells us what to think, feel, and wear.

Sometimes poets say it very well. Poet William Wordsworth says:

> Getting and spending, we lay waste
> our power.
>
> Little we have in nature that is ours
> . . .
>
> We have given our hearts away.[9]

We don't want to be controlled by outer social pushes. Simplicity is a spiritual practice that allows us, in all of our daily activities, to let the Light be our guide.

Queries about Simplicity

What are the obstacles,
frustrations, and irritations in
my life that keep me from living
peacefully and simply?

Do I know when to say "No"
to invitations, committees, and
activities that take time away from
my priorities?

How do I understand my needs
and my wants, and how do I
thoughtfully acquire possessions?

Chapter 4: The Peace Testimony

The Peaceable Kingdom[10]

The wolf also shall dwell with the lamb, The leopard shall lie down with the young goat, the calf and the young lion and the fatling together; and a little child shall lead them.

Isaiah 11:6 (NKJV)

Friends oppose and refuse to engage in war and violence. In pursuit of lasting, sustainable peace, they seek to eliminate causes of violent conflict, such as poverty, exploitation, and intolerance . . . Our work addresses its root causes by forthrightly and nonviolently confronting evil and oppression, We are called to transform the institutions of society into instruments of peace and to be ourselves transformed.

American Friends Service Committee

Whether in times of war or times of peace the Quaker is under peculiar obligation to assist and to forward movements and forces which make for peace in the world and which bind men together in ties of unity and fellowship.

RUFUS JONES (1863–1948)

AT THE VERY CORE OF QUAKERISM, AND at the core of most spiritual practices, is the desire for peace. We want Inner Peace and World Peace. It's a big order and seems impossible to achieve and overly idealistic to some people.

Quakers are one of the three historical Peace Churches, which are known for their refusal to fight in wars. The others are the Mennonite Church and the Church of the Brethren. Some denominations, such as the United Church of Christ, include peace as part of their Statement of Faith. "We believe in the power of peace, and work for nonviolent solutions to local, national, and international problems."

Since the Society of Friends began in the 1600s, most Quakers have been pacifists. Quakers have a long history of opposing war and being conscientious objectors. They have been jailed and even killed for taking this stance.

That doesn't mean that Quakers never serve in the military or in law enforcement. General William Palmer, who founded the city of Colorado Springs, which is near my home, was a Quaker. General Palmer was also a very committed abolitionist. He had to weigh his Quaker stance on the Peace Testimony with his passion for eradicating slavery which was one of the goals of the Civil War.

Learning to be a pacifist is a process. William Penn, as a new Quaker, asked George Fox, the founder of Quakerism, whether he could continue to wear his sword and still be a Quaker. Fox replied, "Wear the sword as long as thou can." George Fox was not making light of this conflict that is inherent in this difficult decision to be a pacifist. Fox recognized that learning to live this Peace Testimony was not easy and it would take some time for William Penn to be comfortable without the defense of a sword by his side. And Fox was right. There came a time when Penn could no longer wear the sword in good conscience.

There are many valid reasons why it can be difficult for non-Quakers to understand this approach. They could ask Mr. Penn, "But you didn't have a Hitler to deal with. What are you going to do about him?" Yet, the 1600s in England had plenty of bad guys—there were the hangings and the beheadings and the massacres and the abuse and the manipulation. All of our ages seem to have plenty of evil. Fear and hatred are not the possession of just one age.

The Leap of Faith

There is a great deal of inner work that goes into coming to terms with this difficult testimony. It takes a leap of faith. It takes a recognition that just as we prepare for war, study war, and invest in war, we need to do the same work for peace. Both warmaking and peacemaking take work and money and a belief and faith in the rightness of that position.

Peace seems impossible on the surface because conflict seems to be deep-seated and many reactions to conflict are violent. But pacifism is not passive and peace goes far beyond the problem of war. The study of peace and how to achieve it is just as complicated as all the strategies and philosophies involved in conducting war. Just as we study the theories of war, the tactics of war, and the execution of war on the battlefield, the study of peace also takes understanding, strategy, and a long time to figure how to do it.

Diana from Portland, Maine, says,

> The Peace Testimony is complicated for me on many levels. That which we call "testimonies" are single words with complicated meanings, actions, and accountability. The Peace Testimony can mean how we live our lives, or it can mean something much larger about Quaker engagement with the

> world. I have often been disturbed and concerned by Quakers' easy, broad anti-militarism which does not acknowledge the complexities of the world we live in. I believe that the most important way we can each live the Peace Testimony is to be realistic about the violence built into our society, to name that violence, to witness it in our lives, and to speak truth to power. If we are silent, we accept the violence and violate the testimony.

Many Quakers learn how to be peacemakers by studying the nonviolent decisions and actions of great leaders such as Ghandhi and Martin Luther King Jr. as well as the work of many peace and justice organizations. Some of them sponsor Alternatives to Violence classes. We try to notice how the occasion of war builds over a period of time.

The Complexities of Warmaking and Peacemaking

The study of modern warfare, at this point in our history, demands an understanding of peacemaking. And the study of peace demands an understanding of conflict and why it erupts into war.

Colonel Lynn Lee, who is a dear friend of mine and an occasional Quaker attender, explained to me this seeming contradiction.

> In the modern United States' military schools—such as the Army War College, which I attended, and most of the military academies—classes include diplomacy, conflict resolution, peacemaking, and negotiating. We are trained as commanders to be calm in crisis situations, and even to reach across the aisle to people who don't agree with us. Some years ago, there were many peace protestors outside our base. It was a hot day and we brought them bottled water.

In a long phone conversation with Lynn, she explained how inherent in our whole government structure peacemaking activities are:

> The United States government, as well as the United Nations and many other countries, recognize that war is the last resort, not the first. That is why we have ambassadors, why we try to create good relationships between countries. We make trade agreements, and we turn to diplomacy first, far before the first shot is fired.

Those who study war and those who study peace often come to the same conclusion: the roots of violence are often based on fear. George Fox saw that we needed to get to the root and the source of where conflict begins and deal with it before it explodes. He said Friends are called to "'live' in the virtue of that 'life'_and power that 'took away' the 'occasion' of all 'war.'"

What is the Occasion of War?

Violence and war never just happen. It's like planting a garden, but instead of planting the peace garden, the war garden is planted and takes some time to bloom in a profusion of chaos and conflict. We need to understand there is evil in the world and there are aggressors who are territorial, self-righteous, pugnacious, quick-tempered, and have no interest and no skills in making peace. This is true for our inner conflicts and irritations, our relational conflicts, and our relationship with other nations.

Quakers try to keep their ear to the ground, listening for the rumblings and looking for the smoldering conflicts beneath the surface before they erupt. They look for the seeds of violence and try to address it when the conflict begins and before divisions and self-righteousness and malice get out of control.

We might first try to notice when our inner spirit is irritated, frustrated, off center, or out of sorts. Why are we nervous? Why are we fearful? Why do things in life seem awry? When do we need a personal attitude adjustment?

In relationships, we try to notice the clues that something is wrong between ourselves and somebody else. We try to notice the spouse that spends a certain amount of time crying privately in a room. We try to notice the child that won't discuss anything anymore or the sharp words that weren't there before. We notice the ways that one person shuts down another person. We notice repression, suppression, oppression, depression. These are all signs that indicate something is not going well.

In most situations that explode into violence, there were clues that were either overlooked or ignored. As one of my Quaker Friends said, "You don't have to be Egyptian to be the Queen of De-Nile."

Almost every mass shooting in the United States had clues of a mental illness, guns in the home that were not secured, police not following up, threatening behavior, or threats made online. Sometimes in school mass shootings, protocol was not followed, whether by locked doors left open or security personnel not doing their job. These are the occasions in social structures that can allow violence to happen because we are not alert, or we are denying that there is a problem that needs to be addressed in its early stages.

Almost all wars begin with threats. Troops gather at the borders, and people try to deny that they're going to invade. The seeds of war are planted way before the first bullet is fired. World War II grew directly out of the unfair treaties that ended World War I. There were years of problems with Hitler before he gained absolute power.

Nonviolence as a response has to be creative and practical. It is not about standing back and refusing to recognize and respond to a threat. It is not about throwing up our hands in helpless confusion, believing there is nothing we can do. It's a different way of training ourselves to react, sometimes counterintuitively. Many Quakers train themselves to respond in a nonviolent way, recognizing that just like a violent response, it may or may not work.

There is a story of a Quaker and a non-Quaker who were talking about the effectiveness of a nonviolent response. The non-Quaker said, "When others become nonviolent, I will then be part of that movement." The Quaker said, "Then you will be the last one to be a peacemaker, but I want to be the first one to be a peacemaker."

Probably many of us fall into some kind of a middle place.

It is easier to ignore and deny than to deal with the full range of emotional nuances and layers of history that are part of any conflict. The peeling away of the problem to get at the core is a long process. We need to deal with our role in it, the role of the other person, the intricacies between two or more people, and the impact that a small conflict has as it ripples outward pulling more and more people into its web. That's a ton of stuff and it takes a certain skill set, processes in place, insight into psychology, diplomacy, a willingness to get the problem out in the open, and a mutual desire to deal with it.

What's Fear Got to Do with It?

One of the main sources of conflict seems to be the fear of what the other person or the other nation will do to us. We have our value systems—such as freedom, equality, our way of life, democracy—and we believe they are worth protecting and even fighting for. Others seem threatening to these values, and often we don't recognize they have their own set of fears and values. The work we do to develop our inner calm often prepares us to lower the temperature when a crisis or a threat starts developing. We train ourselves to pull back rather than to push forward to diffuse the situation.

I find my Quaker calm has served me well in various crises situations. Some years ago, I was going through the checkpoint between Ramallah, which is in Palestine, and Israel. The checkpoint took about fifteen minutes to go through and included about five different turnstiles. At the last turnstile, two young men cut in front of me. They didn't push or shove me, but I was surprised since I clearly was the next in line. We entered a small room where there were two female Israeli soldiers whose job it was to check passports before we went into Israel. Since I was behind the men, by the time I got in the room, one of the Palestinian youth was having a very heated argument with the Israeli soldier (I presumed the argument was in Arabic, but it was certainly a language I didn't understand). I wondered at what point the Israeli soldier would call in reinforcements and other soldiers would come in with AK-47s and start shooting in this small room where there was no place to hide. I said a little prayer, "God, am I safe?" I felt the answer as "Yes." I became very calm and realized it was important I not react with panic, which would raise the temperature in the room. I wanted to subtly help diminish the heat.

I also became very observant of the situation. I looked for clues that this would escalate in some way but saw no body language that indicated a physical threat. Just loud voices. This went on for about five minutes. Clearly everybody knew I was there watching, but I was no threat to anybody. I was about three feet away from the young man doing all the shouting.

Suddenly it was over. The two men left. The Israeli soldier for the first time made eye contact with me, smiled at me, and stamped my passport.

When I left, I realized that what would ordinarily have been a fearful situation for me was not. I felt that Quakerism had prepared me not to have fear in what was potentially a threatening situation.

I wondered why this young man had cut in front of me and then started this argument. I remembered somebody telling me Israelis don't want to have any incident in front of Americans. It occurred to me, since it is usually obvious in a foreign country who the Americans are, that this young Palestinian man saw an opportunity to let off steam in a seemingly safe environment in front of an American.

This incident was an occasion for conflict. It may have been that my calm presence cooled everything down instead of heating it up and adding more chaos. The idea is to get rid of the ire, not spread it.

Quaker Processes That Deal with Conflict

Quakers have certain processes in place that have been developed over many years to deal with relational and group conflicts that can affect a Meeting, affect families, and even affect localities. Sometimes Quakers have a Threshing Session, where the problem is stated, and there is time for everyone to say their piece. Quakers sit in a circle—much like the healing circle of Native American rituals. This is a first step of how one structures the interaction so that there is equality and time for each person to speak. It begins by moving away from the hierarchy into a structure that allows consensus and unity to be reached, without one person lording it over another.

Ginger Morgan, formerly a member of the Colorado Springs Friends Meeting and now a member of Madison (Wisconsin) Friends Meeting, explains the process of a Threshing Session:

Threshing is a term used by Quakers to describe one process which Quaker communities use. It balances Friends' conviction that there is "that of God in everyone" with the very human realities of the diversity of opinions, the play of egos, and the variety of personalities and perspectives that comprise any Quaker (or human) community. Seeking "unity of Spirit" often requires that there is an open, honest space for people to speak their questions, doubts, concerns, and disagreements, and to be heard and acknowledged.

The most important decisions are often not easy decisions. Threshing provides an opportunity to lay out and wrestle with very real concerns and thoughts and opinions. Unity is the fruit of deep listening and seasoning; threshing is the "down and dirty" work of plowing, tilling, and weeding that lays the groundwork for the harvest.

> Since any person can disclose Light and Truth, the Threshing Session helps us together seek the Way Opening.

A Threshing Session usually begins with a question or a decision or a concern that is relevant to the whole community. One person clerks the session in order to guide the group process, but that person has the same equality and responsibility as everyone within the group. Sometimes during a Threshing Session, the concern is refocused or reframed. Sometimes the community decides not to proceed with a decision because there is too much conflict around it and decides to "lay it down," which is similar to tabling it.

Problems with Unresolved Conflict

Although Quakers seek harmony and unity, that doesn't mean we are experts at dealing with conflict. Learning to deal with disagreements without violence and heated exchange is a learned process. Some Quakers have developed this skill, and others have not.

Conflict on a personal level can be as simple as a disagreement where each side digs in their heels and holds firmly to their self-righteousness. Moving through this problem takes listening skills as well as the belief in our own potential, as well as the other person's potential, to find Truth and Light. Sitting in Silence often helps us neutralize our irritations and anger. This doesn't always go easily, but it does depend on lowering the temperature, deep breaths, and a desire to find harmony.

When groups or nations are in conflict with each other, in many cases, conflict comes because of an unequal power structure. One group is oppressed and the other group keeps them in line. This can happen on any level of relationships.

When there is conflict, often one group or one person is not listening, and others are doing all the talking, all the commanding, all the taking. This usually means that other people make decisions without collaborating with the people who are most affected by the decision. It's a basic Quaker principle, as well as a feminist principle, that there needs to be input on decision making from those who have a stake in that decision. There needs to be representatives of various opinions. The founding fathers and mothers of America were saying the same thing when they said, "No taxation without representation."

A number of years ago, I took a class on Violence and Counter Violence. The teacher had been an Archbishop in South Africa and had been deported because of his stand against the power structure during the Apartheid era. He explained that much violence happens because one person or group is oppressed. They try to communicate their struggle and distress. First, they begin with a whisper. They try to make their needs and feelings heard and often begin talking softly and diplomatically. When that is unheard, they raise their voices. When that is unheard, they join with other groups suffering the same oppression. They speak louder. They carry signs of protest. They band together. They start shouting. They move to the next step—anger, riots, and smashed windows.

Still, they are not heard or addressed. Soon comes the shootings. The troops gathering at the border. The killings. The destruction. The wars. Eventually there is the awful and predictable aftermath of war: starvation, billions of dollars put into rebuilding, the hatred still simmering, leading to the next altercation or war. The cycle keeps going. The violent garden keeps spreading its weeds. There is no end in sight.

Cathleen from Santa Monica says:

> What the hell was the struggle about? Why the wasted lives? Was it for power? Power for what? Power to do what? The good guys might be on the winning side, but they are also the losers. Many have PTSD or commit suicide when they return from war. Unfortunately, once you are in the fight, you might be put in a position where you violate your conscience. Once you are in battle, the force of it carries you onward.

Seeking God in Everyone

If you believe there is "that of God in everyone," then it follows that you cannot kill another person. Killing is destroying the divine spark that we believe is in everyone. In order to kill, you have to objectify the other person and you have to dehumanize them and put them on a lower level than you. You are good and they are bad. You have the Christ and they have demons. All these ways that we divide people come to the forefront. You have to believe in your superiority and your way of life and your culture and your righteousness. It is difficult to be working on peace within if you are at war without.

This demands the overcoming of the natural instinct of "Us versus Them." The "them" are the people who are not like "us." They are a different culture or race or religion or economic class or sexual orientation or have values different from ours. They are less than us. They are unimportant. They are expendable. They can be collateral damage if needed. Following this Us versus Them attitude, we can easily decide their problems are not our problems. We draw lines. We create boundaries between us and them. We are unable to empathize. Instead, we create a bubble around us because nothing could be worse for Us, than to be like Them.

We Need to Be Carefully Taught to Hate and Love

These divisions exist on many different levels. Growing up, we see someone who is disabled, perhaps in a wheelchair or with crutches or blind or with an amputated limb, and we don't want to get too close to them because we can't imagine the unbearableness of being in that situation. So we avert our eyes and walk on.

We subconsciously think like this in a number of situations. How could we possibly talk to the homeless because what could be worse than wandering on the streets and trying to sleep on concrete? How could we bear to get close to immigrants asking for asylum? It's too awful to have no money, to have to leave your country because you are threatened physically or economically, and to be rejected as you seek new opportunities and some kind of happiness. Getting too close to the awful realities of life can feel like it's simply too much for us to handle. So we find a way to push it back. It takes a tremendous amount of courage and faith and love to be able to look at the realities that some people are forced to face.

We learn to create all sorts of defensive postures to protect ourselves. We learn to hate people of the other political party or another race or religion or people who dress differently or people who are simply a contrast to us. We pick at the little things that differentiate us. We zero in on them. We blow them out of proportion. Anything that can make Them less and Us more is fair game.

Reversing this means we see Them as equal, and we see God within them. This step doesn't just bring us to being a pacifist and therefore antiwar, it brings us into action to work toward creating a world without war. We seek a different world and we realize that social justice issues are part of creating that world and are a natural outcome of seeking the Light.

The Peace Testimony is about more than just war.

Genie Durland from the Denver Mountain View Meeting says:

> The Quaker Peace Testimony is not a testimony about no war, no violence; it is a Way-of-Life Testimony and so the other testimonies tend to be subsumed within it as one lives it out. Quakers have always understood that war and violence arise out of injustice, discrimination, abuse, marginalization, etc. Understanding that makes it easier to see what I must do to 'enact it.' It means adopting a lifestyle that puts me closer to those who live in the margins, and to actively witness to justice for the victims of oppression and dispossession.

Can Nonviolence Be Effective?

There are many examples of nonviolence being more effective than fighting it out.

World War I killed ten million people. World War II killed thirty-eight million people. As I write this, Ukraine, Israel, Palestine, and Russia—as well as other countries—are suffering from massive destruction and high numbers of casualties. It is difficult to know what nonviolence might have to do with this tragedy.

And yet, even on a global level, nonviolence has been effective in many situations. More than twenty countries have won independence through nonviolent mean India won independence in 1947, Poland in 1989, and South Africa in 1994 when black and white South Africans were allowed to vote together for the first time. There was the Orange Revolution in 2004 when Ukrainian protest led to the defeat of a Kremlin-backed candidate for president. There was the Velvet Revolution in 1989, also called the Gentle Revolution, a nonviolent transition of power that led to Czech Republic's conversion to a Parliamentary Republic.

This approach takes as much training as learning war and can be just as time-consuming if not more so. Ghandhi and Martin Luther King Jr. spent years addressing the roots of violence and training people to resist the oppressors but not to become like them.

There are many who say nonviolence works in some situations, but not when ourselves or our families are threatened. Yet there are many stories of people being talked out of carrying out a violent threat. It is by no means a 100 percent effective—nor is anything else.

Bill Durland, from Mountain View Meeting in Denver, has been in several life-threatening situations and managed to talk the person out of their intention. He says, "It took me over ten minutes or more to calm the person down so he or she could hear what I said."

There is a story about a Quaker who was accosted by a man with a gun who threated to kill him. The Quaker said, "I haven't hurt you and things must be really bad for you if you want to kill someone you don't know. Would you like to go across the street for a cup of coffee and talk about it?" The potential robber said yes.

Some of this talking someone down depends on not moving into the threat but giving the other person a lot of space in hopes of diffusing the threat. It is very difficult to stay calm when threatened and to call on one's inner peace to see if the threat can be diminished rather than raising the temperature.

Some Quakers would consider self-defense acceptable. Diana from Portland, Maine, says:

> I have a black belt in Kung Fu and Kempo Karate and have taught self-defense classes. I never saw it as a non-Quakerly activity. Self-defense is generally reactive, not aggressive. Self-defense skills build confidence, speed, quick thinking, and require physical fitness. Nothing about that is problematic to me as a Quaker.

Like Diana, I took karate at the same time I was becoming a Quaker in 1970. The one time I felt threatened on a street, I immediately went into the karate self-defense position which seemed to be enough for the guy to back off. As Diana mentions, the confidence and quick-thinking that is part of the martial arts sometimes helps diffuse the situation.

Quakers might ask, "How do I create the inner peace that does not fall into fear in a conflict situation? How do I learn to diffuse conflict rather than throwing more fuel on the flames?"

Learning Nonviolence

The path to nonviolence, what is sometimes called conflict resolution, is a slow unfolding path. A number of Quaker colleges, as well as other schools, such as the University of North Carolina and Cornell University, have majors where a student can concentrate on these peace and conflict studies. There are also classes and conferences on Conflict Resolution, the Ethics of War and Peace, Peace and Security, and even how gender has begun to change how we look at creating a society of peace not war.

Quakers have a lobbying group in Washington DC called Friends Committee on National Legislation that meets with congress people to discuss various bills and give the Quaker perspective which might impact their vote.

They have been in the forefront of many Peace movements, such as supporting conscientious objectors and influencing the United States government to accept Conscientious Objectors to War as a valid religious response. My husband, Peter, applied for C.O. status during the Vietnam War. Like many others, he did alternative service and worked for several years at a hospital for handicapped children.

Where Does the Light Lead Us?

It is natural for Quakers to move outward into social action and social justice issues which are all involved, in one way or another, in removing the occasions for conflict, fear, and hatred. Quakers are involved in many different ways of expressing this Peace Testimony.

They have been involved in teaching and advocating for wartax resistance, believing that if we are pacifists, we should not be paying for war through our taxes. It's a form of nonviolent civil disobedience. For some Quakers, such as Bill and Genie Durland of Mountain View Meeting in Denver, they felt led to reduce their income below the taxable level in order to not participate in financing war.

Others are involved in seeking peace in the Israeli-Palestinian conflict. It's not unusual for Quakers to be involved in many different social justice issues. They take part in peaceful protests. They write letters and articles and books. They become delegates to peace and justice conferences around the world.

Bill Durland, now in his 90s, has been a peace and justice activist for many years. He clarifies his long journey:

> I became a Christian pacifist in 1970, committed to civil disobedience for conscience's sake. That included working

with issues such as war, guns, torture, healthcare, environment, simplicity, equality. I was following the truth of Jesus and his best followers, such as St. Francis of Assisi and Dorothy Day, founder of the Catholic Worker's movement. I founded a Community of Creative Nonviolence in 1971.

I had no struggle with the Peace Testimony as it applied to myself. I entered community, I lived simply, I fostered equality and my truth was based on these Quaker Christian values. I helped to create the first environmental state organization in Virginia in 1965 and the first women's course at Purdue University in 1973. I was a peace candidate for Congress during the Vietnam War.

Genie and I were Christians first, then peace activists, and ultimately Quakers. There were many times when we had this huge light of realization in a specific calling

> to one place versus another. In my case it was to decide between a political career or to follow a religious calling, which led me to a different place. I lived at Pendle Hill, the Quaker Retreat Center, for a time as their Justice and Peace teacher.
>
> Genie and I confronted Quakers when I discovered that wealthy Quakers had investments in South African Apartheid, and in warmaking and weapons development corporations. The Palestinian conflict became an issue for me in 1983, thanks to Genie, my wife, and our first trip to the Holy Land. Subsequently, we became involved with Christian Peacemaker Teams.

Bill combined a law career with a PhD in Philosophy and Theology. Like many Quakers, his calling changed over a long period of time.

Genie Durland says:

> This kind of activism enabled us, over the years, to deeply personalize our witness by making friends with the people—Palestinians, Israelis, military personnel, IRS agents, victims of extreme poverty, people on the street—so that we never felt detached from those we hoped to help. In many ways, this understanding of the Peace Testimony demonstrates how it is essentially the basic testimony under which the other testimonies fall. It is the partner to the Truth Testimony in that adherence to and acceptance of the truth enables one to grasp the causes of violence and injustice and try to embrace a lifestyle that avoids complicity with those things.

Protecting the Peaceful Center

We all make choices about where we want to put our focus. We can't do everything, but we can do something. There is a place in our world for those who focus specifically on issues of peace and try to live out this commitment to nonviolence. Quakers hope that this space for the peacemakers becomes bigger and expands. We would hope to influence the ways that we deal with these difficult social issues, so that nonviolent approaches are learned, are tried, and are part of the strategy for how to solve social problems. We believe that peacemaking space needs to be considered as viable and potentially as effective as other approaches, and eventually, to be able to be part of discussions and strategies. We continue to make this commitment to this Peace Testimony, even when it seems impractical.

Creating a just and peaceful world and a just and peaceful people is the goal. Peace Within and Peace Without.

Queries about Peace

How do I nurture Peace within myself, my neighborhood, my country, and the world?

How do I help temper and understand conflict and be a mediator and reconciler when there are disputes?

How do I learn to listen to the other side without irritation and anger or fear?

Chapter 5:
The Integrity Testimony

Quakers before the judges of the English Court[11]

For Friends, having integrity means being authentic and having consistency between one's values and one's actions. Lack of integrity separates us from our own soul, from the Light within, and from our community. We deal honestly and fairly with colleagues and partners. We take responsibility for our actions and their results. We fulfill our commitments, and we give credit to others for their contributions.

American Friends Service Committee

Do not fear truth, let it be ever so contrary to inclination and feeling. Never give up the search after it; and let me take courage, and try from the bottom of my heart to do that which I believe truth dictates.

ELIZABETH FRY (1780–1845)

INTEGRITY CAN BE DEFINED AS AN integration of inner values and outward actions. What we say we believe needs to be manifested in the world. Sometimes this testimony is called the Truth Testimony or a Testimony about Honesty. We try to tell the truth as we know it. We try to be authentic people and be truthful about our flaws and our mistakes as well as our strengths and our gifts. We endeavor to live in the Light and turn to the Light to lead us as we make important decisions. We work at being honest and fair in all our dealings with others. We understand that a harmonious inner life should be leading us to bring harmony and peace and goodness in our world.

What Is Truth?

In John 18:37–38 in the Bible, Pontius Pilate asked Jesus this question: "What is truth?" He was clearly grappling with his feeble conscience because he could find no reason to crucify Jesus. He asked a philosophical question but he did not wait around for the answer. Instead, he went out to the crowd and let them know he found no fault in Jesus. But he clearly felt the pressure of the establishment Jews and of the mob. He went against what he knew to be true and instead gave the crowd the choice to release one man to them as was the custom. Would the crowd prefer Jesus or Barabbas, a robber, murderer, and rebel condemned to death by the Roman authorities? The riled-up crowd also had lost their conscience and chose Barabbas.

Jesus mentioned several different qualities of truth. He said the truth would set us free. And he also said with his death, there would be an advocate that would help us find the truth and help us stand with the truth. "And I will ask the Father, and he will give you another advocate to help you and be with you forever—the Spirit of truth. The world cannot accept him, because it neither sees him nor knows him. But you know him, for he lives with you and will be in you" (John 14:16–17 NIV).

Quakers, as well as most spiritual groups, would look at this advocate as the Holy Spirit, or the Inner Light, that enlightens everyone. "But the Helper, the Holy Spirit, whom the Father will send in my name, he will teach you all things and bring to your remembrance all that I have said to you" (John 14:26 ESV).

In Quaker practice, truth is not laid in our lap like a creed or an absolute. We sometimes struggle to find the truth. We sometimes are uncertain how to express the truth. But this testimony clarifies our commitment to the truth.

Some years ago, I was a member of a Friends Meeting where one of its members was in jail. Several of us from the Meeting visited him during that time, and on the day of his release my husband and I volunteered to pick him up from the jail and be available to him for the day. When he came out of the jail, we asked if he would like to go to breakfast and he said, "Yes." We had a nice long breakfast at Denny's. We went grocery shopping. We moved a few of his things in my truck. Then he told me he needed to go see his parole officer that day. I took him and asked if I could also be in the meeting. He agreed, as did the parole officer.

During the meeting, the officer turned to my friend and said, "What was the first thing you were supposed to do after you got out of jail?"

"Come here," my friend replied.

The officer said, "And what did you do instead?"

My friend recounted all the things he was not supposed to do first. I had no idea he was not following orders. After the meeting, my friend and I got in my truck and I said to him, more forcefully than my usual self, "You're a Quaker and you're supposed to tell the truth and you did not. You cannot do your parole this way. Tomorrow, when you see the parole officer, confess and take whatever punishment he gives you and tell him the truth. Also tell him you're going to be the best parolee he has ever had. Commit to being honest with him." My friend got through parole and refound a good life.

Committed to the Truth

Truth can shift. But we are committed to the truth although there can be difficulties about how to apply the truth. Truth can be stubborn and difficult to discern.

Quakers have struggled with the consequences that can occur when someone tells the absolute truth. They sometimes ask, "To what extent do I hold to the truth with such ferocity that my truth might cause harm to others?"

During the time of the Underground Railroad, Quakers were at the forefront of helping escaped slaves which is, at its core, a deceptive thing to do. Abolitionists were hiding slaves, taking an illegal action, and in many cases were put in a position where lying would save the slaves and telling the truth could lead to recapture or perhaps even death. If they told the truth, they were in danger, and the slave was in danger. If they said they were not hiding slaves, they were telling a lie and compromising the Truth Testimony.

What did they do about this dilemma?

In some instances, they trained their children to hide the slaves but not tell them where they were hidden. They would give food to the children and say, "If you know of anyone who needs food, give this to them." Of course, the children gave the food to the slaves. When the slaveowners asked if the parents knew where slaves were hidden, they could honestly say "no." Or they could say, "Not that I can see," as they looked up at the sky, which was still truthful.

Quakers pondered whether misleading others was compromising this testimony. Can we hold so tightly to the actual words of the truthful text that we are lying in the subtext? Are we so careful of the words that come from our mouths, that we are lying in our hearts? Or are we trying to be so truthful that it seems we're "splitting hairs"?

Diana from Portland, Maine sees truth as complex:

> The truth looks very different to different people based on cultural norms, history, and starting assumptions. From the time I was old enough to think about these things, I have understood that integrity, truth telling, telling partial truths, withholding information, and telling untruths is very, very complicated. I have chosen to deal with this complicated area by not attempting to draw bright lines, because I don't think they can be drawn.

There is a Quaker joke about our commitment to the absolute truth. Two men, one of them a Quaker, were looking at a herd of sheep grazing on the hillside. The non-Quaker said, "What beautiful sheep. Isn't their wool just magnificent?"

The Quaker replied, "Yes . . . at least on this side."

Quakers Seek a Single Standard

Quakers take this testimony into every aspect of their lives, including their businesses. In the early years of Quakerism, as some Quakers became merchants, there were often two standards of pricing. The buyer and the seller would haggle over the price of goods, and depending on who did a better job of haggling, the seller might lower the price. Sometimes parents would send their children to a store to buy merchandise and the seller would take advantage of the child and raise or lower the price, depending on the circumstances.

Of course, there are many societies and cultures where haggling is the way buying and selling works. Quakers however, believe in a single standard of pricing. You set the price and it doesn't matter who buys it.

When I began my business as a script consultant, I had to decide how to apply this value. Some of my friends suggested I have one price for studios and production companies, since they supposedly had lots of money, and another price for writers, who usually had less money to spend. After some pondering about this, I realized this idea was not based on the truth. There are writers with a lot of money and there are film companies who have small budgets.

I decided to follow the Quaker practice of a single standard of pricing. I created a number of different services. If a studio or individual wanted more detail, they would pay more. I also decided to be very specific about what each service included and provide the same quality of work for everyone. I stayed within the boundaries of what I had set and advertised. If someone ordered the service that included twelve to fifteen pages of notes, I didn't do ten pages or seventeen pages just because "I felt like it." I always tried to be clear about what the client would receive and make sure there were no surprises.

Fair Business Practices Means a Fair Exchange

Most of us who have careers that work with the public recognize this is a relationship that presumes a certain amount of honesty between buyer and seller. The buyer doesn't try to slip counterfeit bills into the transaction when paying. The seller doesn't try to cheat the customer by adding water to the soda or by hiding bruises on the apples. A good business transaction is an exchange of trust as well as an exchange of money for the product.

Integrity sometimes means recognizing when the exchange is off. This fair exchange includes paying fair wages to employees, as well as asking for fair wages for ourselves. We don't demean our work by underpricing our worth.

We try to live within our means and don't pretend that we are richer—or poorer—than we actually are. Certainly, there are people who make a show of wealth they don't have—sometimes spending beyond their means. And there are people who pretend they don't have money in order to get special treatment.

In my thirty-nine-year career as a script consultant, I occasionally refunded money to dissatisfied clients—which were very few. In the beginning of my business, I automatically refunded money if my client asked me to, because I wanted my customer to be satisfied. Over the years, I realized there was another layer of mutual integrity when someone asked for the refund. Just as I took my work seriously, the client needed to take my work seriously as well. Some clients would read a critical remark in my report and immediately ask for their money back without reading the whole report or applying the solutions I had suggested. This was unfair to me and to them. Eventually, I decided that integrity demanded that they take the report seriously before asking for a refund. If they were dissatisfied, I suggested they read the report three times, breathe deeply, and apply the advice to their script. If they felt the script became worse rather than better, then I would refund their money. It was interesting to me that in several instances the client apologized profusely after they followed this direction and got past their emotional response. I was insisting on integrity on their part as well as integrity on my part.

The Refusal to Swear Oaths

Part of this commitment to truth was expressed through a refusal to swear an oath such as one might swear in court or as part of a contract or an oath of fealty to somebody else. The founder of Quakerism, George Fox, was asked to swear an oath of allegiance and to recognize the supremacy of the English King. In 1663, he told the judges, "It was Christ's command that we should not swear. Our allegiance does not lie in oaths, but in truth and faithfulness." George Fox took the Bible verse about oaths very seriously. In Matthew chapter five, followers of Jesus are commanded, "Do not swear an oath at all: either by heaven, for it is God's throne; or by the earth, for it is his footstool; or by Jerusalem, for it is the city of the Great King. And do not swear by your head, for you cannot make even one hair white or black. All you need to say is simply 'Yes' or 'No'; anything beyond this comes from the evil one" (Matthew 5:34–37 NIV).

Quakers believe that swearing an oath means that you have two different standards of truth. One standard is in your normal everyday life, where you might fudge, fib, stretch, or deny the truth and make false statements. The other standard is saved for the witness stand where you promise to tell the whole truth. Instead of swearing the oath, Quakers sometimes say "I affirm," meaning they affirm that they will tell the truth under all occasions.

Historically, Quakers were hauled into court many times and thrown into prisons for this belief. They continued to keep telling their truth, as they understood it, even under difficult circumstances. Even now, on those occasional times Quakers are in court, many will simply say, "Yes" or "I affirm."

Modern Quakers have different attitudes about swearing oaths. Trevor Benda, who lives in England and is part of a British

Truth and Integrity Quaker group, says, "I think Quakers in Britain would routinely decline to swear an oath in court. This is regarded as quite normal."

In the United States, some Quakers continue to refuse to swear an oath and sometimes there have been legal consequences to that choice.

Bill Durland from Denver Mountain View Meeting says, "In 1975, while a peace activist, I was arrested and asked to take an oath or affirmation but I took neither and told the Court that I would follow Jesus and simply say 'yes' or 'no.' And so, I was convicted of a misdemeanor."

I personally had to decide how to express this Integrity Testimony when I began to do expert witness work in the area of copyright infringement. Not everyone in the film business has high morals and it is not unusual for producers to have seen somebody's script and used it as the basis for their film without compensating the writer. Writers go to see the film and say, "That's the character I created. That was my story. There's even some of my dialogue in that movie."

This may or may not be true. Just because two characters in both script and film are in love and kiss on the beach while the sun is setting does not mean the one stole from the other. We might only look to our own life to know there is nothing highly unusual about that. However, if it just happens in both script and film to be on a beach in a small town in Oregon and it's a mixed-race couple and she happens to be the only lawyer in this small town and the man is the son of the mayor—well, one begins to think there might have been some infringement here. Sometimes similarities are this clear, other times they are more subtle.

The lawyers for both the writer (the plaintiff) who is suing and the defendant (the producers) both need to hire an expert on screenwriting to analyze specific similarities and decide whether they're so unique that two people probably would not have come up with this same idea.

This work as an expert witness meant that I would be deposed and also testifying in court to give my opinion on whether there was infringement. This meant taking an oath. As a Quaker, I had to decide whether to take the oath and say "I do" or to use the Quaker term, "I affirm." I pondered this as Quakers often do when they need to make a decision on how to follow the testimony within the complexities of their own lives. We hold the testimony up to the Light and figure out how it can guide us when making this kind of a decision.

I spoke to the lawyer who had hired me and explained I was a Quaker. We discussed the possibility of saying, "I affirm," and he was willing to go along with my affirmation, but he knew it would cause confusion for the jury. He said he would cover this confusion by causing a distraction at that moment so the jury would be looking at him, not at me. I felt the core of this testimony was to tell the truth with clarity and accuracy. I decided to call a Clearness Committee of Quakers to discuss this. I felt my responsibility was to my work and to the case and I could see no benefit in confusing the jury.

I took the historical attitude about the swearing of oaths seriously. Yet it seemed to me that following this refusal to swear an oath would cause more harm than good. Quakerism is not a legalistic religion, and when we seek the Light, we might make different decisions than other Quakers might make. We ponder, weighing the situation and the consequences, we hold it up to the Light, and then we make a decision.

But What About the Integrity of the Other Person?

Just as the Light reveals the truth, the Light can also reveal when we are at fault as well as when others are at fault. So many of us try to be so tolerant and so non-judgmental that we might end up not looking clearly at the truth. There is bad stuff in the world, which is sometimes called evil or the shadow or the gray areas.

Some people are dishonest. They lie—in person, on social media, in religion, in politics, and in their relationships. They tell little white lies and big whoppers. They justify and defend their lies. They cause all sorts of problems and harm to other people. What do we do about it?

We sometimes fail to recognize that other people have a different standard of truth. We may cling to the idea that others will see our standard and change, when it just isn't going to happen. Or we might not recognize relationships can be dishonest and that we have the right to disengage.

This issue of integrity brings up the questions: "When do we confront the problem when someone is dishonest and doesn't pay us, or lies about us? How do we confront it? When do we decide not to confront it? How do we analyze the benefit and the harm that might result?"

Our confrontation of the problem could cause harm to us in many ways. We might never get paid. It might harm our reputation, or break up relationships we believe we need to get ahead. It might redefine us among our colleagues who then believe that we're a problem and hard to get along with. It might change what we believe about our own identity and what others believe about us.

Confronting the problem can also harm the reputation of others. What do we do when we confront the dishonesty in another person and word gets out that harms this person's reputation? When do we publicly speak up and when do we stay silent?

This is a time we might have a Clearness Committee. You don't have to be a Quaker to call together a small group of wise friends known for their listening skills and good advice. I have a very dear friend who is not a Quaker that I often call on when I need wisdom. Her responses usually fall into two categories. Sometimes she'll say, "You need to confront this, because this is a problem affecting more than just you. It's affecting your career or the people you serve and it might even be entangling other people in a way that isn't fair to them. You need to speak out because no one else will." Other times she'll say in her Texas drawl, "Don't get none of that on ya." Sometimes there is no benefit to anyone to get in the midst of the yuck. A situation can be toxic and it's best not to get involved.

In most religions this is called "discernment" or "wisdom" and it has a great deal to do with these delicate boundaries. Truth is not just an individual issue, but is also a relational and social issue.

Living by the Rule of Threes

Integrity asks us to fine-tune our ability to look at ourselves and create a standard of truth, and be willing to look at the world through that standard. We don't want to be blind-sided or taken advantage of because we don't see the truth about the faults within ourselves and others. If we are blind-sided once, we don't want to keep being taken advantage of. At the same time, we want to be just, merciful, and tender with each other.

I have learned to use the Rule of Threes, which a sitcom writer taught me: "You set up the joke, you develop the joke, and then you pay it off."

Here is how the Rule of Threes work when things are not so humorous. This can keep us from being entangled over and over again when somebody is not truthful with us.

The first time somebody is rude or mean or dishonest, notice it. It might be a simple mistake. Give them the benefit of the doubt if possible, but take note of it. The second time, consider that this may be a pattern. This means noticing when someone does something bad to someone else, as well as when they do it to you. This is often the time to confront it and have a good heart-to-heart talk with that person. Sometimes this is the time to just wait. But the third time tells us it's an ongoing pattern. It might be time to disconnect and disengage and not "get any of that on ya." Or you might decide to still work with that person but be wary and don't let them have power over you.

Forgiveness comes when others ask for it or when we have to disconnect but forgive the other within ourselves. Sitting in the Light can calm us down enough that we can begin to see what to do and have the courage to do it.

It's important to see the truth of the situation before addressing it. The Rule of Threes helps us see the pattern fairly clearly without getting stuck in the pattern over and over again. It can also show us ways to address and resolve the problem.

Truth Can Be Brutal

There is a natural resistance to hard truth. This can be particularly true in medical professions. Diana was a nurse for many years. She says,

> Working as a nurse, there have been many, many times when I was confronted with moral issues that were at least partly about integrity. As nurses, we protect the patients, but if the doctor makes a mistake, we're not supposed to

> tell the patient what happened. I often found that what happened is not the same as what was reported to have happened, something over which I had no control.
>
> I also found that sometimes I had to be 'brutally honest,' as some would describe my approach. People often have serious misunderstandings about what it means that a disease is fatal 50 percent of the time, or that a drug works 10 percent of the time. I would be very clear about what that meant, and not give false hope, because that had already been done. I would often apologize for being so honest, and usually got a response that indicated that the person was relieved to hear the facts in a straightforward way."

Although the truth can be brutal, knock us off our center, and demoralize us, the way we tell the truth can still be gentle. Difficult things can be expressed with grace and tact and an understanding of the emotional truth of the person hearing the hard truth.

We can train ourselves to ask for and accept the hard truth. Doctors and pastors and teachers and others might be resistant to telling us that we have a serious illness, or that we have crossed some moral lines, or even that we did not deserve the "A" that we were begging for. If we're committed to the truth, we might need to develop this skill of being tender with ourselves and others.

Telling the Truth Can Have Consequences— Some Good and Some Bad

Sometimes we don't know the consequences of telling the truth, but we stay committed to the truth anyway.

Once when I was asked to be an expert witness, I had been persuaded to accept a case because the screenwriter had done a convincing analysis of the similarities between his script and a film. After I started working on the case and accepted money for my work, I began to have an increasing realization that I hadn't looked carefully at the details and my assessment was wrong. I had put too much stock in his analysis, and not enough stock in doing my own independent work. This was not a good idea.

I decided to withdraw from this case because my integrity did not allow me to continue down this path. I called the lawyer I worked for and apologized profusely for my mistake. I took full responsibility for my incorrect analysis and offered to return the money they had paid me. I felt terrible about the breach of trust I'd committed. I also had some fears I would never again work in this field once word got out about what I had done. But it was clear to me this was the right thing to do, because I could not defend this case in court.

I expected the lawyer to heave a big sigh and say something like, "Oh no! What are we going to do?" But he didn't say that. I was amazed by his reaction. He told me he had great respect for the courage it took to stand on my integrity. I discovered later that their firm withdrew from the case as a result of my decision. There is no way I could have expected this reaction or these consequences, and yet it seemed to me, in retrospect, that my decision of integrity may have led to them recognizing a truth about the validity of this case.

Giving Credit Where Credit Is Due

Honesty is related to the idea of seeing clearly. We give credit to others for their contributions. We don't take credit when it's not due to ourselves and we don't inflate other people's accomplishments.

Integrity means we try to assess others fairly and accurately—when hiring or firing or choosing to be collaborative partners. We try to separate our hopes and our projections from a clear analysis of reality. We try to be wise about these assessments, taking responsibility for the decisions that we make in our business relationships and personal relationships. Spiritual people, who are loving and kind, can often try so hard to be tolerant, that they sometimes don't call behavior out for what it is. There can be plenty of abuse, bullying, immoral behavior, and toxic people—even among communities that claim to love each other. We try to see clearly.

Integrity means we don't embellish our own accomplishments. Sometimes people try to raise themselves up by association with people they consider to be above them. Sometimes they make up information about other people, giving more credit than where credit is due. They hope by raising the other person up and by being close to them, they also will be raised up.

In my business as a script consultant, some people told me, "You're better than Wonder Bread" and "You're the #1 person in our field," and "You're better than your colleague." Friends and colleagues sometimes told other people falsehoods about me which sounded good but were simply not true. One of my colleagues often said, "Linda works with all the big studios and with all the major directors like Steven Spielberg and Ron Howard." Not true. I always tried to correct her and set the record straight. I worked with many new writers and occasionally famous ones, but not with Steven or Ron.

In many industries, there is "ego getting out of control" and the embellishment of resumés. Some people say, "Well, everyone fudges a bit." No, everybody does not. Our accomplishments are our accomplishments and don't need to be enhanced nor diminished.

This also means standing up for ourselves when people try to demean us. We try to be aware of our own gifts and try to be aware of those times when someone tries to make us less or more than we truly are. They might tell a falsehood about us, which we correct. They might refuse to give us credit when it's important that a boss or an associate knows where an idea has come from, or who has made a particular statement that can then be followed up. We might think credit is all about ego. But many times, credit is about telling the truth so a project can move forward, and the creator of the idea can be a valuable ongoing resource.

Standing up for truth also means standing up for others who are being disrespected. Sometimes we discover there has been an injustice done to a group of people and we might band together in community to address the injustice. That is the core of social action and it's the core of the meaning of community. We have a responsibility to the truth as it affects us as a group, not just the individual.

Truth in the Public Arena

In this time of "fake news," disinformation, deception, Artificial Intelligence generating false content, social media repeating lies, and political corruption, Quakers and many other religious groups recognize that truth is not just about our individual integrity, but needs to be addressed in the public arena.

In Great Britain, the Quaker Truth Testimony is the focus of the Quaker Truth and Integrity Group (QTIG). Both Jan Arriens and Trevor Bending are part of that group. Jan explains their goals as:

> Promoting truth and integrity in the public arena. We are attempting to do this in a positive way, i.e., commending good practice rather than highlighting abuses. Sometimes this involves weighing

up a number of sometimes conflicting considerations. In terms of QTIG, the concentration is very much on public affairs rather than personal conduct. Integrity and trust are closely bound up with each other. They also have a fundamental bearing on the way in which society operates. This is all the more important at the present time, with the enormous challenges we face in the world. For instance, unless we can confront climate change honestly and consistently, short-term self-interest will prevail—to the detriment of us all.

Integrity and trust are also bound up with cooperation and getting beyond individual self-interest.

I see this as a major next step in the evolution of humanity—one that we will probably not adopt wisely in advance but one that will be forced upon us by the calamitous consequences of climate change and the ensuing strife and violence. The

> Quaker truth testimony therefore has a vital role to play in the future ordering of human affairs.

Trevor sees truth as covering a number of social areas, including:

> Scientific truth but also political, historical, factual truth, and the difference between right and wrong, so I suppose moral truth.

This can also include a balancing act between being open to the ideas of others without being easily swayed by passion and fervor. In a civil society, we hope to remain civil, which sometimes means committing ourselves to thinking and pondering policy, and looking for solutions that consider the emotional truth of people who hold firmly to positions. This is not always a matter of compromising, but might be a matter of the creative third possibility that sometimes comes from holding an issue up to the Light.

For many Quakers, this means being aware of oppression in society and the negative influences that are considered "all right" by some. Quakers see discrimination as a false assumption that some people are not as equal as others and are not deserving of equal rights. This might seem to be part of the Equality Testimony, but they see their social justice as part of the Truth and Integrity Testimony as well. These are social conflicts that must be addressed. Trevor says:

> I've always stood up in particular for the 'underdog.' I think this is relevant today in terms of our attitude to race, immigration, and discrimination on any grounds.

Our commitment to social justice is a commitment to recognizing that social contracts and constitutions and statements of what a state and country believe in need to be acted out in society. If we say, "All are created equal," we need to follow that statement with laws that are enacted and respected. Just as our individual inner truth needs to be expressed outwardly in all of our relationships, trust in a country's government depends on the government fulfilling its promise to what it says it believes and values. Social contracts, even when they are not explicitly spelled out, need to be followed or a society falls into chaos.

Where Does Faith Come In?

Telling the truth takes faith, because we have to believe and have faith that the benefits, whether in the short or long term, make the world a better place. We need to have trust in the consequences of truth telling and to abide by the truth even when we don't know what the consequences will be.

If our lives are dependent on adjusting our truth to get a certain consequence, we might be very wrong and the lie ends up not working the way we expected it to. We think it's going to benefit us or somebody else, and it actually turns against us instead. Our truth telling contains an element of faith. We believe that our lives and the world is a better place and a more just place when truth prevails and when people stand on their integrity.

Queries about Integrity

How can I gently and clearly speak my truth to those who agree with me as well as those who disagree with me?

How do I harmonize my inner life and my outer life so they are consistent with each other?

How do my beliefs and values line up, and are my spoken words and my actions consistent with my values?

Chapter 6:
The Community Testimony

Wandsworth Quaker Meeting[12]

When Friends gather in silence to worship, they are collectively seeking the will of God, rather than meditating individually . . . in gathering together, people increase their strength, vision, wisdom, and creativity.

American Friends Service Committee

Membership is, or ought to be, about transformation. The transformation of individuals who have experienced the divine spirit at work in their lives. The transformation of a community which has sensed, and tries to live out, its particular role in bringing about the transformation of the world which can be seen as God's purpose.

HELEN ROWLANDS[13]

WE MIGHT THINK THAT SPIRITUALITY IS about what is going on within us. We try to be good people. We meditate and pray. We tune in to the Spirit to get direction and to feel a connection.

In most religions, there is a recognition that spirituality is not just within us but between us. Something happens as we gather together and as we recognize the bonds of connections. This is different than what happens when we are alone in solitude doing our own individual spiritual practice.

This Spirit also leads us to express our spiritual lives with others. We try to care about our neighbors. We try to do what we can to make a better world.

Saint Paul's Definition of Community

In the Bible, St. Paul traveled from one community to another to nurture the new church. Most of them had many internal struggles. He scolded and cajoled, confronted and comforted, pushed and encouraged, trying to help these new communities understand not just their individual connection to God, but the sacred connections that are formed when the Holy Spirit gathers us together.

St. Paul recognized that it takes many different kinds of people with different gifts to make up what he calls "the body of Christ:"

> There are different kinds of gifts, but the same Spirit distributes them. There are different kinds of service, but the same Lord. There are different kinds of working, but

> in all of them and in everyone it is the same God at work.
>
> ~1 Corinthians 12:4–6, (NIV)

In Romans he continues this same thought:

> For as in one body we have many members, and not all members have the same function, so we, though many, are one body in Christ, and individually members one of another.
>
> ~Romans 12:4–5 (ESV)

Each gift that the individuals bring is important, and no one gift is more important than another. These gifts are seen as God-given and need to be nurtured by the community so they work for something beyond just the individual.

> Now to each one the manifestation of the Spirit is given for the common good. To one there is given through the Spirit a message of wisdom, to another a message of knowledge by means of the same Spirit, to another faith by the same Spirit, to another gifts of healing by that

> one Spirit, to another miraculous powers, to another prophecy, to another distinguishing between spirits . . . All these are the work of one and the same Spirit, and he distributes them to each one, just as he determines.
>
> ~1 Corinthians 12:7–11 (NIV)

The community cannot work as a whole without each part being engaged and responsible and connected. This is even more true with Quakers because there is not one authority figure who leads them or pulls them together. Each individual has the responsibility to contribute and let their voice be heard.

Seeking Community—How Does the Spirit Unite Us?

We form communities based on shared values, often shared belief systems, and shared relationships, which might be forced on us but nevertheless bind us together. Not everybody likes their families, but they keep meeting together at holidays and are determined to strengthen those bonds even when there is a whole lot of rubbish between them. There are many people who have been part of church communities for decades even though, in private, they might say, "I really don't believe much of this, but this is the church I've been going to for years." Not all communal relationships are good. Some of them need to be reassessed.

The core of a communal relationship can be quite different for different groups.

A number of church groups, such as Evangelicals, base their communities partly on shared belief systems. It isn't unusual for an Evangelical to ask, "Are you a believer?" The correct answer in their view would be, "I believe in Jesus Christ as my personal savior." And they emphasize the individual relationship with Jesus and how that is shared within the community.

Quakers rarely ask each other about their belief systems. That is not what binds us together. There are many Quakers who identify as Christian but will talk about their Christian belief systems in different ways than other Christians might. Some will say, "I believe Jesus is a very good man and a model for us," and identify as Christians. Others will talk about the Christ within and others will talk about how they see Jesus and the ways in which they follow Him.

What we have in common as a Quaker community is not so much a belief system, but an experience, and a faith that the Light is accessible and can be found within each of us, within the other, and between us. That doesn't mean Quakers have no outside authority and they do what they want. Historically, the Bible has informed much of Quaker life. Quakers believe that the guidance we receive from the Inner Spirit does not contradict the Biblical authority that tells us how to live good lives. When we follow our conscience, we believe it will not contradict what we know about moral norms and what it means to love each other. We are to question any time the guidance we receive seems to be mean-spirited, abusive, justifying violence, or destructive. There is nothing godly about diminishing others, committing violence, or raping the land.

Community Expands Our Identity

If we are truthful about who we are and who we want to be, then we will usually seek out a community that makes us more authentic people as a result of the community's influence on us and our influence on them. Many Quakers come to Quakerism as a result of negative experiences with other spiritual communities that demanded certain belief systems and unquestioned obedience. They want to be able to be truthful about what is going on in their spiritual life and they want to learn how to nurture and expand it.

We would hope that the communities that attract us would be communities that nurture the Holy Spirit within us and the Spirit between us. We would hope that a spiritual community is a safe place to be.

Becoming more involved with a community often leads to changes in our identities. Some of these changes we might not want, although it may take some time to realize the community has a negative influence on us. If so, we might change communities to help us find or expand our authentic identity.

I grew up in a fairly liberal Lutheran Church, so I was solidly part of a church community. It gave me a sense of belonging and acceptance. I learned much from the prayers and sermons about how to apply my faith to daily life. I became enriched by certain stories in the Bible since every week there was an Old Testament reading, a reading from the Gospels, and one from the Epistles.

I also learned a certain freedom to explore and seek. When I was sixteen and could drive, I would go to the 9 a.m. Lutheran service, and then I would try out another denomination which had an 11a.m. service. I found I liked the quieter services of the Methodist and the Presbyterians better than the more liturgical services of the Lutherans, Episcopalians, and Catholics.

In my 20s, I wanted a more personal relationship with God, I wanted to learn more about the Bible, and I wanted a more personal active prayer life than the more formal prayers I learned in church. So, I switched communities. I more or less fell into a Bible-based literalism and took on another identity as a Fundamentalist and an Evangelical. This stage lasted for three years. I learned to fit in. I learned the vocabulary. I knew the Bible verses I was supposed to quote. I knew not to question. But as I became more involved, the many authoritative people in that group began to frighten me with their judgments and all of the restrictions. As a woman entering a career, I really had trouble with the idea of women submitting to men and of men being superior.

During this time, I kept a journal. When I reread the journal, I felt like I had become a little robot, and I was losing my identity rather than gaining it.

When I came to Quakerism in 1969, I began to feel something happening within me. I realized that one of the things I liked about the Methodist church was the few minutes of silence they had in their service. The Quaker Silence set well with me.

I also liked the way Quakers interacted with others without the defensiveness I was feeling inside of me. I found, on the whole, that Quakers were not self-righteous. I discovered that I could keep my relationship with Christ and even my belief in Christ as my personal savior in the midst of this community that included some people who were not Christian. I could continue my Biblical learning. And because the Quakers were tolerant, I could continue to be respectful and loving in my relationship with friends from other denominations and other faiths. I knew that world and I did not have to reject it, but instead I could recognize my need for a different kind of community that I felt would nurture me for many years.

Quakers seemed to accept doubt and valued the questions as much as they valued their own personal spiritual experiences that connected them with God. There is a Quaker saying: "This I know to be true." They recognize that in a healthy community, one's experience of God opens people up rather than closing them down.

We are enhanced rather than diminished. We become bigger people through the embrace of the community.

Community Includes a Shared Vocabulary

When we enter into a community, we enter into a certain framework. This framework has its own vocabulary, although a good healthy community doesn't try to limit us by vocabulary, but tries to expand our way of thinking. If we're not comfortable with the vocabulary of the community, we probably won't stay there. The words for God that Quakers use, such as the Light Within, the Divine Spark, the Source, hopefully feel good to us and enrich us.

Quakers use phrases such as, "sit with it" and "season it." We follow the Light "as the Way opens." George Fox says, "Walk cheerfully and gently over the earth, answering to that of God in everyone and everything." All of these words and quotes either feed us or they don't.

The community affirms who we already are while still influencing us as we grow into a new identity that now includes our Quaker faith and practice. Sometimes when new people come to a Quaker meeting they say, "I've been a Quaker all along—I just didn't know it." They have found their spiritual home.

The Gathered Community

A community is not just a group of individuals sitting together in silence and having their own individual experience of the Spirit. Something happens that is not the same as sitting in solitude. There is a sense that there is a movement of the Spirit between us that connects us with each other and that brings us into unity.

Quakers do not prepare a message before coming to worship. We speak out of the Silence when a message comes to us and there is a stirring within us that tells us this is a message to be shared. We got our name "Quakers" because Quakers would shake when that fervor came to them and let them know that their pondering was not just for themselves alone. Quakers often say they feel a push and sometimes a nervousness before they speak. Some ask God at that moment, "Do I really need to share this?"

"Yes, you do."

Messages are usually short: three to five minutes long. They are not a response to a previous message. They are not conversations or reactions to what has been said. Often, we have been pondering about some issue or idea or concern in our daily life, and it takes form because we are sitting in that silence. We are moved to share the message and it seems other people are on the same page.

Messages in many Meetings do not have a direct connection to each other. But sometimes something happens where it feels as if the messages gather together on a similar theme, as if we are going down the same path during that Meeting. Quakers call this a "gathered community."

I have sat in a Meeting before, and at the beginning I have had a thought that has a certain amount of energy and clarity to it.

But I didn't feel moved at that point to share this thought. I sat with it and continued to season it. Then someone stood up in the Meeting and had a message that was related to the thought I had. It wasn't as if we both saw the same news story. It was an unusual synchronicity. I continued to sit with my thought but wasn't moved to share it. Soon someone else stood up and their thought resonated with a previous thought. It's as if the Meeting was moving in a similar direction. I sat longer. Another thought was shared and again, it was not a direct offshoot of what had been said before, but it was clear we were swimming in the same sea. There was a feeling that this issue had been working its way through the hearts and minds of a number of us. Then I felt moved to speak, and I realized that my ponderings were meant for the end of Meeting, not for the beginning.

Although this is most apt to happen when the messages follow a theme, sometimes Quakers will feel this sense of a Gathered Meeting even though nobody speaks. The silence seems to be particularly rich and our connection to each seems particularly strong and loving.

Gerald Hewitson in *Journey into Life* describes it as: "A meeting where the silence is as soft as velvet, as deep as a still pool; a silence where words emerge, only to deepen and enrich that rich silence, and where Presence is as palpable and soft as the skin of a peach; where the membrane separating this moment in time and eternity is filament-fine."

It doesn't happen every Sunday, but when it does, Quakers would say the Spirit is pulling us together into unity.

Seeking Unity

Just as the Spirit pulls us together during worship, Quakers also seek this same kind of unity in their business meetings and committees. They use a form of consensus.

The common understanding of consensus is agreement by everybody. There are a number of nonreligious organizations and even some corporations that will occasionally use this form of decision making. Everyone involved in the decision has to agree with the solution in order to proceed. This removes the possibility that somebody in the group will sabotage the action because they didn't agree with it.

Quakers take this a step further. It isn't just a matter of everybody agreeing. In other organizations, sometimes people say they agree because they don't know how to explain why they disagree. Sometimes they say they agree because they feel overwhelmed by the group. Quakers believe that individuals within the group should feel "at ease" with the decision and in unity with a decision and the action to follow. If one person in the decision-making group is uncomfortable, Quakers believe that person's discomfort might be important and may be coming from the Spirit. Since Quakers believe in the equality of everyone, it is the responsibility of everyone to share their discomfort.

Sometimes no decision is made because there is not agreement. Sometimes the person disagreeing "steps aside," meaning they respect the agreement of the rest of the group and might not totally agree with it, but they don't want to be in the way of this decision.

Unity is not achieved by a vote. We seek the will of God, not our own will. We believe the Spirit unifies rather than divides us.

During a business meeting or a committee meeting, after some discussion of the issue, the clerk of the Meeting discerns whether unity has been reached. The clerk might say, "I believe we are all in unity" and the members of this Meeting nod in agreement if that is a true statement. Or the clerk might say, "We don't seem to be in unity on this issue," and call for a moment of silence. This silence might bring clarification or raise new questions or new solutions. If unity is not reached, the issue might be saved for a later date or simply tabled until someone feels like bringing it up again.

The whole Meeting is seeking the Light and believes that the True Light will bring them together.

The process of unity works on big issues and small issues.

I was the clerk of one Meeting where we were deciding whether to buy a small church building which would then become our Meeting house. We had been renting space for some years and finally were ready to have our own space. The building we were considering had some problems, but we thought they were solvable. I thought we had reached unity to proceed. However, the building did not pass inspection so the sale did not go through.

Later, two members of the Meeting told me they were adamantly against the purchase but they had not said anything. I wondered how I had missed their discomfort. It was partly my responsibility as the clerk to be attuned to the group. It was everybody else's responsibility to be absolutely honest about how they felt. The problem was not the Quaker process. The problem was the expression of the process.

When my term as clerk ended, the new clerk continued the process of looking for a space. This new clerk was highly skilled and experienced. She had no greater voice than any of us, but she knew how to make sure this process was followed with great care and respect for everybody. We found another church building which met our needs well and we found unity in this purchase.

This kind of decision making can work in small ways as well. My husband Peter and I were members of the Santa Monica, California, Friends Meeting for many years. Shortly before we moved to Colorado, someone in the Meeting suggested that we put up a Peace Pole in front of our Quaker Meeting House. Peter was against it because Quakers do not use outward forms to express their beliefs—such as a cross, an altar, vestments, or stained-glass windows. As a result of Peter not agreeing, the Peace Pole was not put up at that time. We moved to Colorado and returned for a visit to Santa Monica some months later. There was a Peace Pole in all its glory, right there in the front of the Meeting House. Obviously there had been another meeting and everyone had agreed. There is a Quaker joke that says sometimes a person has to move or die before a decision can be made. We moved. They decided.

How Is Unity Reached When There Are Problems in the Group?

The unity found in this form of decision-making demands that each individual develops an ability to seek the Light.

Sometimes we have a bad feeling about something. Maybe we feel we have been taken advantage of. Or we feel someone is dishonest with us, but we can't put our finger on it. Sometimes we feel we are being a sucker.

I have been a member of a number of different Quaker Meetings in the last fifty years, and I've learned in most Meetings there will be some problematic people. Often, a Quaker committee called Ministry and Oversight is assigned to deal with this problem. This takes discernment and discussion. How do we do good to people who are not doing good to us? How do we recognize deception and manipulation while still being available to be of help and try to engage the Light within that person? What is really going on with this person and where can we be of help and where are we not able to help? How do we understand our part in the problem and take responsibility for that, and how do we recognize when we are being manipulated?

I've sat on several Clearness Committees which were formed because a person in the Meeting stood up and played some part of the Blame Game: "You people in this Meeting are not Christian. I keep asking for help and you don't give it to me. You're not doing what Quakers are supposed to do." The Blame Game can include nuances that are truthful and force us to look at our individual selves and our particular Quaker Meeting, but sometimes this person is repeating a pattern that they have followed with many other groups over the years.

One person in a Meeting I attended for many years tested the patience of other Quakers who had tried to help him. He became a toxic presence at the Meeting and resisted all efforts and all processes that we offered. His demands were unreasonable, sometimes bordering on the ridiculous. He thought we should buy him a car and give him an airplane ticket to move to Florida to be with his partner. We didn't buy him a car, but one member of the Meeting had enough reward miles to buy him an airplane ticket. He went to Florida and came back within two weeks—with a new set of demands. I suddenly had a realization and a moment of clarity. I turned to him and said, "Why do you continue to come to Quaker Meeting when you don't like us and don't like the way we do things? You don't like the way we try to help you. Nothing we do seems to be good enough or acceptable. Why don't you go to a group that you like?" After that, he only came to Meeting when there was potluck, which was fine with us. We continued our kindness but recognized both his limits and ours.

Recognizing manipulation and deception by sitting in the Light can give us wisdom about what is really going on.

We Need Each Other—the Community Fulfills the Need

Community doesn't just happen in worship. A good community nurtures and supports one another. It's easy for us to feel self-sufficient. It's easy to feel that we don't want to inconvenience others or to be dependent on others. But we need each other. We have the ability to impact each other, help each other, even save each other in times of crises and tragedies. We are vulnerable and often fragile human beings. The good that each of us does can ripple outwards and bless others and change the world, and the bad that is done can also ripple outwards and hurt others and the world.

Many Quaker Meetings, if not all of them, have a committee called Ministry and Oversight (M&O) or sometimes Ministry and Counsel (M&C) or Pastoral Care. This committee's job is to look after the spiritual health of the Meeting. That means that anyone in the Meeting can come to them with a problem and the committee tries to help them find some solution or resolution.

Some have Meeting House Committees that deal with the care of the meeting house. When a Meeting is planning on building or renovating a meeting house, they will usually have a Building Committee that deals with the decisions involved in creating a meeting house design, including the particular needs of the group, the finances, and reaching consensus on the issues with the entire Quaker Meeting. When a committee has fulfilled its purpose, such as a Building Committee, it will then be laid down.

Some Meetings have Social Action Committees and do outreach to the larger community. Sometimes this means that Quakers get involved with other groups, such as Justice and Peace organizations. Sometimes a small group of Quakers will have a presence at a protest or work with other groups involved in social justice. In certain cases, the Meeting reaches unity that certain members will represent the specific Quaker Meeting when they become involved with a social justice group.

My husband and I were founding members of the Colorado Springs Sanctuary Coalition. Other founders included the United Church of Christ and the Unitarian Church. We established a safe place within the Unitarian Church where we could host people who were in danger of being deported, even though they had lived in the United States for decades. We co-hosted the Sanctuary guests, which meant vetting the people who desired sanctuary, coordinating with their attorneys on what was needed, and providing food, laundry service, visits with their families, and companionship. Over a period of several years, we had three different guests who took refuge in the church, sometimes for several months and in one case, for a year. The coalition worked together to find unity on issues and decisions that came up during this time. Later, the committee expanded to include other immigrant rights. We tried to keep the Quaker Meeting informed about our work and about the coalition.

All the committees work to reach unity on any decision. Sometimes this takes much discussion and wisdom to know what to do about certain problematic issues.

Helping Without Being Manipulated

Some years ago, I was on the M&C committee. The Meeting had just completed building a caretaker's room so somebody would be able to live at the Meeting House full time. The person who was going to become the caretaker had not yet moved in.

One of our frequent attenders came to our committee, asking if she could live in that caretaker room for two weeks. Her situation on the surface seemed fairly simple. She had just finished her PhD and was offered a job in Europe that fit beautifully with her area of expertise. We were excited for her. But there was a problem. She was very attached to her cat and could not take the cat with her. Her attachment seemed a bit excessive to many of us. We understood the love that people that have for their pets, and we tried not to judge, but we were worried that she would give up this amazing career opportunity for her cat.

She had a number of conditions for whoever would be a good owner for her cat. The cat was positive for feline leukemia so it couldn't go to a place with other cats. She also didn't want her cat to live in a rural area. Nor did it seem that any of the city offers were acceptable.

Her new job was to start in two weeks and she had to be on a plane on a certain date. But she didn't want to leave until her cat had the perfect home. She had become so obsessed with this cat and so anxious about it that her current roommate evicted her.

The M&C committee considered her request and recognized the layers of this situation and why a whole lot of people at the Meeting were irritated with her. Our job was to try to help her make a wise decision, but not allow her to manipulate us. We decided to offer her the space with the condition that she had to move out on the day that her airplane left. Furthermore, she could not bring the cat with her to the caretaker room because the carpet in that room was new and we didn't want to take the chance the cat would scratch or cause other problems while living in that room. We also felt, even though we did not mention this to her, that it would be very good for her to sit in solitude at times to meditate and reflect about the career move that she might be giving up. This would give her the opportunity. She accepted our conditions.

She found a temporary place for the cat for those two weeks. The day before she left for Europe, she stood up in our Quaker Meeting and thanked us for the opportunity. She said she had plenty of time to reflect and realize that she had gotten her priorities very mixed up, and that this time alone had been very good for her in order to see the Light. We didn't have to tell her. We just provided the space, hoping that the silence and time would help get her on a good path. The temporary home became the permanent home for the cat, and it all worked out just fine.

M&C in this case had to think through the layers together and reach unity on how we would handle this and what our hopes were for her. Of course, they were her hopes as well—she just had to go for it.

What Tears Us Apart?

It is not unusual for a spiritual community to be stretched at the seams and be tattered and torn over personality conflicts or other issues. In my experience and in my research, I have noticed three different issues that have sometimes split Meetings or caused people to leave the Meeting.

The first situation that often divides a Meeting are social issues. During changing times, social issues arise that ask Quaker Meetings to take a stand. Quakers have often been ahead of the curve with issues such as women's rights, immigrant rights, civil rights, conscientious objection to war, and LGBTQ+ issues. That doesn't mean the individual Quakers are all at the same place, and there can be disagreements on how to handle a social issue.

During the Vietnam war, many non-Quakers were attracted to Quaker worship because they knew Quakers were pacifists and had taken a stance against the war. People who had no prior experience with Quakers would come to worship because they saw the opportunity to have "their say" in a safe space. Their messages would often express their anger at the war.

While there is certainly room for this in a Quaker Meeting, some of these people had come just to vent as opposed to sharing a message that had come from an Inner Light. They might stand up and speak for a long time. Or their anger would feel threatening to others worshiping. Meetings became disruptive and chaotic. Sometimes Quakers responded within the Meeting with a gentler message. Occasionally a clerk would interrupt an angry message and say something like, "Dear Friend, this is not our way," or, "Dear Friend, we have heard you." Sometimes the person was "eldered," which means they were taken aside with a gentle clarification about what worship was about and what was appropriate and not appropriate.

The second thing I've noticed that can divide a Meeting is money. Some Quaker

Meetings have encountered turbulence when they are suddenly given large amounts of money. Perhaps somebody died and the Quaker Meeting was a beneficiary in the will. Everyone has an opinion about what to do with this money—and sometimes their opinion has a great deal of intensity. This is an opportunity for Quakers to show their values and do Good Works. But there can be many different ideas about what those Good Works might be.

Conflicts often arise when a Meeting is planning to build a new Meeting House or build an addition to the Meeting House they have. Everyone has to be on board, and yet this is a time when some people don't care whether rooms are added or not, or they have a vision that is particularly strong about what needs to be done. In two instances which I know about, someone in the Meeting felt a Leading for remodeling. A leading such as this, which involves the whole community to be in unity, needs to be tested with the whole community. In both cases, the whole community was not on board and the person who felt this leading started pushing and even pulling other members to get them on their side. This is not the Quaker way and it is a risky place for everyone in the meeting

The third thing I've seen is that one person's Leading can potentially divide a Meeting. Leadings which are genuinely guided by the Spirit need to be taken seriously, but these Leadings need to be tested with the community because they involve the whole Meeting and large amounts of money. It is a risky place for everyone in the Meeting. There are times that people start taking sides, and suddenly the Meeting is divided rather than unified. It often takes great skill from the clerk of a Meeting and the calmer and wiser people in the Meeting to step up and recognize the danger. Some are running without fear toward their vision and others are left with a choice to disengage or to confront a vision that needs more discussion and decision-making. In all cases, for unity to be reached, there needs to be tender loving care. When passions are high and desires are out of control, this can be a difficult process.

The Bonds of Community Respond to Each Other's Needs

Many churches and many Meetings have Hospitality committees. When somebody is sick or in the hospital, they let others know and might even schedule visits or food to be delivered. The M&C Committee will often be asked to organize a response to a need. Sometimes this committee even oversees money that is given to help a fellow Quaker member.

When my Quaker friend Cathleen—whose name you have seen in this book—had cancer, three of us from Quaker Meeting banded together to make sure she had the help she needed. She needed food; people to go to chemotherapy with her; people who would take her ten-year-old son to and from school, baseball practice, and Boy Scouts; and even several of us who helped her son bake the cake that was needed for his next Boy Scout event. Every morning, the three of us Quakers talked on the phone and decided who could do what to take the load off Cathleen so she could focus on her appointments and on her healing.

Shannon O'Connor from Portland, Maine, was on a Pastoral Care Committee for a number of years. She says:

> We would have phone conversations once a week on my lunch hour and just reconnoiter what was going on with Friends, even if there was no dramatic need or crisis to work on. Yet there were often dramatic needs and crises. We would organize food and its delivery, give rides to appointments, and try to respond to each other's needs.

When the bonds of community are strong, what needs to be done is done. When the community is working well, there is that miraculous movement of the Spirit that makes sure there is always somebody there who can help.

Over and over again, through my years as a Quaker, I have been amazed at how the garment that is our community doesn't shred or tear or have holes in it when the community comes together.

Queries about Community

How do I honor the diverse contributions of others and see each person's part in creating community?

What are my gifts? How do I take responsibility and offer my gifts to the community?

Are there ways I disengage and resist these sacred connections?

Chapter 7:
The Equality Testimony

Social Justice Is More than a Brand[14]

Friends hold that all people are equal in the eyes of God and have equal access to the "inner Light." We reject all forms of discrimination, whether based on race, ethnicity, nationality, religion, immigration status, class, gender, age, ability, or sexual orientation. We work to change the beliefs, practices, and institutions that perpetuate prejudice, and examine our own biases and privileges.

American Friends Service Committee

Being worthy of respect does not depend on possessing attractive qualities or skills. Until we can respect another person without justification except that he or she is a child of God, it is not really respect.

PAUL LACEY, QUAKER EDUCATOR

QUAKER FAITH BEGAN WITH THE IDEA that all are equal as God's children. All should have equal rights and equal respect and an equal voice.

If there is "that of God in everyone," not only do we respect everyone, we also help others who are disrespected in their struggle against discrimination, oppression, and rejection. We help equalize the playing field for ourselves and for others. This is not just a democratic principle but a spiritual principle.

The focus of this testimony has changed through the centuries. In the beginning of Quakerism, part of inequality was between the wealthy and the higher-ups versus those on the lower end of the social scale. Quakers saw everyone as equal and therefore did not doff their hats to those of a higher social standing, such as the king and other royalty. Quakers were willing to go to jail to stand by this testimony—and they did.

There can be a very subtle differentiation for each of us in terms of who we consider to be the higher-ups. We can still easily fall into this mindset. Sometimes those with less education believe that those who are more educated are higher-up and therefore don't feel they can easily talk to them. Some people consider the wealthy to be more important than the poor. Some consider the famous to be more lofty.

When we bend our knee and doff our hats to the higher-ups, we grant extra power to them. We see them as somehow more authoritative than others. There are those in our society that rank themselves as lower than others, thereby demeaning themselves and becoming self-deprecating and lacking self-esteem.

Quakers work against this tendency to rank others as more important or less important. This has led them to take part in many different kinds of social movements that address inequality.

From the beginning roots of the Quaker faith, Quakers have been part of civil rights movements. They were instrumental in the beginning of the Abolitionist Movement, the Underground Railroad, Women's Rights, Native Rights, and later, LGBTQ+ Rights.

Since women were leaders in Quaker Meetings, they became natural leaders in other social justice movements. Susan B. Anthony, who came from a Quaker family, was a leader in the women's movement of the 1800s. Alice Paul, a Quaker, worked for women's suffrage and was in the forefront of helping women get the right to vote. She co-authored the Equal Rights Amendment, which has now passed in thirty-eight states and is waiting to be integrated into the Constitution. Lucretia Mott and Sarah and Angelina Grimké were Quakers who were in the forefront of the feminist movement in the 1800s.

Quakers worked for equality in many different areas. Some Quakers, such as Mary Dyer in Boston, sought religious freedom for themselves and others so everyone had the equal right to worship as they pleased. They were often jailed, tortured, and hanged for that desire for freedom of worship. Eventually these reformers were successful, and by the time of the Declaration of Independence and the Constitution, freedom of religion was considered a democratic right.

Some made prison reform their cause, such as Elizabeth Fry, so prisoners had rights. If we believe there is "that of God in everyone" and all are equal as children of God, then we seek justice, and we seek humane care for others. Quakers began to work for prison reform so prison would be a time of rehabilitation. They sought humane treatment and the end of torture and capital punishment, because if there is "that of God in everyone," there's always the possibility of a little spark beginning to glow and finding its way to creating goodness.

Quakers worked for racial justice. One of the few treaties that was never broken was the treaty between William Penn and the Delaware Indians of Pennsylvania. If we believe in equality, we don't take the other person's land and culture away from them. They should have the equal rights we want for ourselves.

When the Iroquois went on the warpath, they often avoided Quaker homes because Quakers kept their doors unlocked and put a white feather on their doors as a sign of peace. The Indians trusted them and sometimes even babysat for the children of Quakers when they went to their yearly meetings.

How Do Quakers Find Unity on Social Issues?

The issues around what we do to help others achieve equal rights, equal respect, and equal self-determination are not always easy. Many times, it takes a number of years for Quakers to find unity on a social issue.

When discussions of how Quakers would deal with same-sex marriages began in the 1980s, many Quaker Meetings struggled with this cultural change. On the one hand it seemed clear that same-sex couples should have the same rights as heterosexual couples. On the other hand, for some Meetings, this was a bridge too far, and they did not come to unity about being in favor of same-sex marriages. Some Meetings split up over this issue and in some cases, those who disagreed formed another Meeting.

I was a member of the Santa Monica Meeting during this time, and we had several gay and lesbian couples in the Meeting. Rather than waiting until we were asked, we decided to have a Threshing Session. This was the shortest Quaker Threshing Session I have ever attended. We asked the question: "Are Friends comfortable with a same-sex marriage if we are asked by any of our members or attenders to be married under the care of Meeting?" We had some moments of silence. We looked at each other. It was clear very quickly that we had all reached unity. This was a natural conclusion from our Equality Testimony. We simply had no problem with it. The Santa Monica Meeting and many other meetings have had same-sex marriages.

Looking At Our Experience

Quakers often process their response to social issues by reflecting and pondering and seasoning where we stand individually on an issue. We might reflect on our upbringing and our prejudices and our experiences. We try to be willing to be honest with ourselves. We try to shine the Light on any innate racism and sexism and any other "ism" that we're exploring.

We sit in silence. We try to illuminate the issue. We read about our Testimonies. We study the history and how others have confronted these Testimonies. We think about where we fall short.

Many of us have stopping places where it's really difficult for us to cross that border and see the other as equal. It is a challenging process to see our place in the problem as well as our place in the solution. Many of us have unconscious biases that are created by our backgrounds.

I grew up in a small all-white town of 2500 people in northern Wisconsin called Peshtigo. We were just about equally divided between Protestants and Catholics. We knew from an early age that Protestants did not marry Catholics. This bias was firmly in place.

We had one Jewish family in town. The woman was a very good friend of my mother's and one of my favorites of her friends. She was smart and wise, and from my very limited data, I developed the stereotype that "all Jews are smart."

I remember the first time a black person drove through our town, and I and all my little girlfriends lined up and stared, as if a Martian had just zoomed past.

When we went to Milwaukee to visit my grandparents, we had to drive through the black section of town and mother would quickly say, "Lock your doors!" I learned that those black people were dangerous. We were to protect ourselves against them.

Mexicans came for the summer to pick cucumbers since there was a pickle factory in the nearby town, and I quickly learned they were a different class than us, and that they would leave after the summer was over and go back home. We had almost no interaction with them.

Often, we begin our journey toward a recognition of everyone's equality by noticing those places where we stop and move back or avert our eyes rather than moving forward and engaging.

Usually, these prejudices begin with outward physical appearances—such as seeing a person of color, or a person who is disabled, or who wears different kinds of clothes, or performs different kinds of rituals. It can also include the moment of realization when we understand the person thinks differently than we do, has a different value system, or doesn't believe what we believe. We might think our values are basic human and universal ideas. It shatters our world view when we realize they are not. A boundary is established to "protect ourselves," and soon a great many people become The Other.

I discovered through my simmering with this Equality Testimony that I simply did not know how to talk to people who were different than me and outside my experience. It seemed on the surface to be so simple—but it wasn't. If I moved forward toward the person in order to establish contact, hoping to overcome my prejudice, it seemed I was overcompensating. If I moved back too much, out of uncertainty about how to engage, it seemed I was rejecting this person. I realized I was not seeing this individual as a person, but as a category. I was objectifying the person in order for me to practice getting over my innate biases. People who grow up in multicultural contexts probably have far more ease communicating than those of us who grew up in a homogenous culture.

I met my first transgender person in 2016. Misty Plowright had given a speech at the Democratic County Convention in

Colorado which was quite powerful. But I had trouble adjusting to the voice that came from this person and I couldn't figure out the gender. It played a brain game with me. Ordinarily I would have gone forward and told Misty that I loved the speech, but I hung back. When I saw Misty again, I decided to go forward but then felt like I was in the mode of "practicing," and I didn't like that, but I wasn't sure of another alternative for me to learn what I wanted to learn. But that was another of my stopping places—and this Testimony led me to tell myself, "Get over it!"

In the musical *South Pacific,* there is a song "You've Got to Be Carefully Taught" which talks about how we're taught to hate, to fear, and be afraid of anybody who is different from us. For many people, it's not natural to have these boundaries. We have to be taught by our relatives and parents and teachers and friends if they hate somebody, we're supposed to hate the same people—and we're usually taught these lessons as very young children.

Fear and uncertainty drive these attitudes. We are afraid of what those "Others" might do to us. We have little understanding of their lives and are fearful that the more we understand, the more vulnerable we are to recognizing that we too are the "Other" to them. We learn to categorize and create boundaries. We judge and justify. The "wrong side of the tracks" is not just an analogy about trains.

A Process for Pushing Ourselves past Our Boundaries

In Quakerism, there is a relationship between inner reflection and outward action. After we reflect and ponder, we then might ask, "What can I do about this? How can I help?"

These issues are not just individual issues. They are social issues. A natural movement of this individual reflection leads to involvement in local, national, and international responses. It's not unusual for groups of Quakers to go anyplace on the globe where they witness injustice and inequality.

We try to move from the concept that "nothing foreign is human to me" to the concept "nothing human is foreign to me." We seek the Light so we can begin to understand the nuances of our attitudes and how they were formed by our experiences.

Maggie from Portland, Maine, discovered some of these biases that she and her husband did not even know existed when they adopted a biracial child. Maggie says:

> The Equality Testimony is very close to home. Thirty-four years ago, we adopted a biracial child. We had a white pediatrician who was afraid that we would not take Casey because he was biracial. We thought nothing of it and welcomed our beautiful baby boy into our home. But my husband and I were surprised by our white privilege attitude, despite having someone so close to us who was biracial. We thought that we would be free of any prejudice, but had to admit to each other, that when we saw a black man with a hoodie, walking

> towards us, we were nervous. Black meant different and what was worse, dangerous. We kept hoping that we could erase this attitude but it was so ingrained in us that we had difficulty doing so.
>
> Our son, thankfully, is colorblind. He has many friends that are black. He doesn't seem to suffer from confusion about who he is which often happens with biracial children.

Even if we grow up in households that taught us to respect those who are different than us, we might continue to be challenged by all the nuances of this Testimony.

What Actions Do We Take?

As we reflect on our unconscious biases, it is a natural progression to ask the question, "What can I do about these?" This question can lead us to look for places of discrimination or inequality which can sometimes be overt and sometimes subtle.

We often look to what is within our sphere of influence.

I entered the film industry in 1979 after reading a booklet, *Window Dressing on the Set,* (United States Commission on Civil Rights, 1977) about the negative depiction of females in film and television. I began to see how often the roots of inequality in our social system come from the role models that are presented to us in the media. Women were not well-represented—either on the set or behind the set. Women's roles were often defined by their relationship to men—as wives, mothers, the love interest, or the sex interest. I wondered if I could make an impact by moving forward with this leading.

I joined several women's organizations, including Women in Film. I attended conferences, wrote letters and articles, and helped female colleagues get jobs. In the mid-1980s, I became chair of a committee that was part of Women in Film. Our goal was to create an award that would recognize movies and television shows with positive depictions of women. Since I was the chair of the committee, as a group we decided to organize based on the consensus model that Quakers had used from their inception. This helped the committee become very unified and very respectful of each other. But, it didn't help when we had to work with the board which was based on more of a hierarchical model.

We named it the Luminous Award and created criteria for how to judge a film. The awards were presented in 1986. We received a great deal of positive press for the ceremony. Some of the presenters at the award ceremony included Betty White and Valerie Harper. The success of this ceremony led us to brainstorm ways to expand our reach. We planned to do short presentations for executives at studios and production companies on how to recognize stereotypes and to help them change how their movies depicted women. Unfortunately, one of the producers on the board of Women and Film had produced a film that didn't win. It became a political mess and the award was discontinued.

In 1995, I was a delegate at the United Nations Women's Conference in Beijing, China, and attended several discussions about the depiction of women in the media. I realized the work we had done for the Luminous Award over a three-year period was very forward thinking. We could have brought this whole international discussion to another level if we had been successful. Because the award was discontinued, we weren't able to have the impact we could have had. As with any social issue, there is often defeat, but we continue nevertheless. Today, great progress has been made in the area of women's equality and to some extent in the depiction of women in the media as well.

Addressing Other Inequalities

Like sexism, issues of racism in its many forms continues to be an area of focus for Quakers. These include issues of self-determination, equality under the law, reparations, and territorial rights.

The Christchurch Friends Meeting in New Zealand has been addressing Native Rights issues. Murray Short from that Meeting says:

> We share the history of the many nations that were colonized, mostly by the nations of Europe. The ideology underpinning colonization was one of inequality and so unsurprisingly, the outcome of colonization has entrenched inequality as evidenced in Aotearoa (the Māori name for New Zealand) by the way Māori are over represented in areas such as unemployment, educational underachievement, life expectancy, suicides and rates of imprisonment to name but a few.

Murray clarifies that part of this is advocating for indigenous rights and self-determination. In New Zealand, some of this means honoring the treaties that have been made with the Māoris, the equitable sharing of resources, and sharing decision-making. In 1995, the Yearly Meeting in New Zealand made a statement about the Māori-Pākehā relationship (Pākehā are

New Zealanders primarily of European descent). The statement recognizes that much of inequality is driven by fear and this needs to be acknowledged:

> We are convinced that there is nothing to fear from the prospect of Māori being empowered to take control of their own affairs and manage them in their own ways. In the words of the United Nations Draft Declaration on the Rights of Indigenous Peoples, "Indigenous peoples have the right of self-determination. By virtue of that right they freely determine their political status and freely pursue their economic, social, and cultural development.
>
> It is not surprising that there should be misunderstandings and breakdowns of communication. We are always heartened by evidence from around the country that these barriers can be surmounted, and satisfactory solutions found to apparently

> intractable disagreements. We call on all people of goodwill to look for reconciliation beyond the confrontations, and on the Government to pursue with sensitivity and vigor its search for the justice in accordance with the Treaty without which there can be no peace.

Another statement was made by the New Zealand Yearly Meeting in 2008:

> We are committed to social justice based on our belief that there is that of God in all people. This leads us to approach all relationships in a spirit of goodwill, fairness and cooperation, which has been a hallmark of the Quaker approach to social, political, business, and international affairs. We believe that social justice is a necessary precondition for true peace between peoples and that this is at the heart of the Christian message.

> The constitutional changes we would wish to see would include power sharing arrangements with Māori both nationally and locally. The task of achieving constitutional change will not be an easy one and requires careful and thorough negotiation.

Cannon Valley Friends Meeting in Minnesota is another of the many Quaker Meetings worldwide dealing directly with Native Rights. They also created a statement for their yearly meetings *Faith and Practice* book that says:

> Mere professing is never sufficient. Northern Yearly Meeting is reaching in and out to experience more fully the deepest meanings of being inclusive and nurturing. We want to recognize and celebrate diversity. We are called to act wherever we see inequality. We want to engage with each other and our wider communities now to create opportunities for this vision of a more just society. Justice

> can only be served when all those involved can understand the consequences and engage with one another to bring positive results into being.

For the Cannon Valley Friends, this meant educating themselves about the problem; sharing books; attending lectures, exhibits, and native pow-wows (called "wacipiin"); and inviting a local indigenous woman to speak about her experiences. The Meeting also looked for other resources—bringing books into their library and watching and discussing a video about boarding schools for native children. They donated money, organized with other faith communities, and built a community among non-native folks in support of their indigenous neighbors.

Just as the Peace Testimony relates to almost every other Testimony for Quakers, the Equality Testimony does as well. It is the basis of peaceful and nonviolent ways of relating to other people. It overcomes our inclination to create barriers. It challenges us and asks us to be alert. This Testimony asks us to learn to be sensitive to the diversity within our social structures and to value these gifts.

Queries about Equality

How do I look for opportunities to lovingly relate to people who come from different backgrounds than mine and who have different belief systems?

How do I work to change myself and society so that all are given equal rights?

What do I do when others are demeaned or diminished or treated unjustly?

Chapter 8:
The Stewardship Testimony

Cannon Valley Friends Meeting
Rain Garden with Peace Pole[15]

Good stewardship means taking care of what has been given, not just for ourselves, but for the people around us and for future generations as well. Friends strive to use their gifts in accordance with their beliefs. Concern for the ecosystem also leads us to strive to reduce our personal consumption and develop a simple yet adequate lifestyle.

American Friends Service Committee

We do not own the earth. Walk gently upon it, so that future generations may do the same.. . .

Walk cheerfully . . . over the earth answering to that of God in everyone and everything.

GEORGE FOX (1656)

THE STEWARDSHIP TESTIMONY WAS ADDED in 2011 and is the most recent. SPICE—the acronym for Simplicity, Peace, Integrity, Community, Equality—became SPICES. If you grew up in a church of another denomination, stewardship often meant charitable giving and supporting the church and its missions. Certainly, there is that nuance with the word in Quakerism, but it has taken on more and more meaning in terms of stewardship of the earth over the years because of the climate crises and the earth in such travail at this time in its history. It was a natural progression. If "there is that of God in everyone," and if we are to extend our care and equality to everyone, it follows that we would also care for the Earth and the Creator who made it.

Although the testimony itself is relatively new, the concern is not. Historically, from the beginning of Quakerism, Quakers spoke about our responsibility to care for the Earth. The Stewardship Testimony challenges us to live up to this practice.

In 1692, William Penn said all of us need to be "better studied . . . in the Creation of [the world] for how could Man find the confidence to abuse it while they should see the Great Creator stare them in the face in all and every part thereof."[16]

In the 1700s, John Woolman said:

> As the man was moved by an inward principle to love God as an invisible, incomprehensible Being, by the same principle, it was moved to love Him in all His manifestations in the visible world. That as by His breath, the flame of life was kindled in all animals and sensible creatures. To say we love God as unseen and at the same time

> to exercise cruelty towards the least creature . . . was a contradiction in itself.

This respect and appreciation for nature is not the same as pantheism. We are not worshiping nature; we are caring for the Earth in the same way that Adam is told to tend the garden. We recognize it as a responsibility. It is not a matter of conquering or subduing nature to our will, it's a matter of being servants. Quakers sometimes call this Earth Care or we call ourselves Friends of the Earth.

Francis Hole in *A Little Journal of Devotions out of Quaker Worship*[17] says:

> It is as if the Divine Presence said to us: "Ever seek balance . . . You are to love and appreciate yourself, other persons, plants, and creatures around you, stars, earth, snow, rocks. Do not 'fall in love' with any of these to be possessed by them and swallowed up; neither turn away from them nor renounce them. In the balance that you

> attain, keep Me ever in view. Each of you is my unique darling, as is everyone and everything around you.

What is the Meaning of Stewardship?

In Quaker terms, Stewardship fits well with the testimony of Simplicity. We try to avoid excessive consumerism, which depletes the Earth's resources. Consumerism takes land, water and fossil fuels for most of our buying desires. Vanity drives the desire to buy excessively. 'Keeping up with the Joneses' is vain and not simple.

Stewardship is part of sustainability. We try to create structures that nurture rather than harm the earth. It is not unusual for Quaker Meeting Houses and Quaker Retreat Centers to strive to be carbon neutral.

This comes partly from the relationship of our inner life moving outward into our social life and into the created natural world. It is one movement and the Holy Spirit continues to expand Its reach. How do we preserve our planet and how do we express our stewardship as our Light moves outward?

In many ways, this question of stewardship is a learning process. It is learning to think bigger. It is learning to educate ourselves about the consequences of our actions as well as our responsibilities. Quakers are part of what is considered the Progressive Movement that links us with all religions and spirituality that are concerned by the greed and exploitation of our planet, and who practice creating a better future for our planet and the people who live on it.

Practicing Our Stewardship Through Our Meeting Houses

Although our numbers are few, we are still building Meeting houses, but building them differently. Concord Friends Meeting in New Hampshire built their new Meeting house in 2010. Ruth and Greg Heath, along with others in their Meeting, were instrumental in trying to create a carbon neutral building.

Ruth says:

> When our Meeting decided to stop renting from a daycare center and build our own Meeting house, we wanted to be sure it would reflect our testimonies of Simplicity and Stewardship of the Earth. Simplicity bids us to conserve energy and use minimal resources. Within our own homes we value energy conservation, recycling, and all means to lower our carbon footprint. We have tried to live as lightly as possible in cooperating with the Earth, even before we were aware of the climate crisis. We do not use plasticware for events, having a good supply of mugs, plates, and silver available, which we hand wash. We only turn on the refrigerator when we need it. We do not use paper towels but small personal washcloths, which are laundered. The Meeting house was built to reflect those values.

In the Concord Meeting House this meant looking at all aspects of the building. Ruth and Greg clarified the building material:

> We built with Earth-friendly materials, used super insulation, and installed a highly-efficient wood-pellet boiler. Therefore, it uses very little electricity and was awarded an Energy Star rating.

This careful planning extended to how the building was placed on the land:

> We sited the building with a southern orientation and gave it a properly pitched roof for solar panels. In 2018, we covered our roof with solar panels. Because we only needed a quarter of them for our building, we created a group net meter project, producing enough power for another three homes. We deliberately did not plant grass, but landscaped with ground cover to eliminate the need for mowing. We are now a net-zero building.

Like other Quaker projects, this was a community endeavor, building on the talents and contributions of other Quakers.

> We were heavily influenced in our plans by our beloved member Don Booth, who was a solar pioneer in New Hampshire. We and other members live in passive solar homes built with Don's influence in the 1980s. We had a service to dedicate the building shortly after we moved in. It was Don's last outing before he died. As he was wheeled into the Meeting room after Friends had gathered, a broad smile filled his face, and his arms and hands were spread wide as if welcoming us to his new home. It's a memory we cherish.

Ruth concludes by saying,

> Building a Meeting house is one thing. Worshipping in it is another. We hope that the Spirit that fills the space fills us as well. We hope that we carry it forward,

> supporting each of us in the small but crucial decisions of our everyday lives.

Planting and Caring for the Garden

Many Quaker Meetings plant sustainability gardens around their Meeting houses. Cannon Valley Friends Meeting in Minnesota created a rain garden when they built their Meeting House in 2013–2014.

Patricia Johnson from Cannon Valley clarified that this was a natural extension of putting the testimony into practice:

> Northern Yearly Friends Meeting (which is made up of Meetings from Iowa, Michigan, Minnesota, North Dakota, and Wisconsin) has articulated a testimony on Care for the Earth since 1988. In 2001, Alden (Mac) McCutchan, a member of Cannon Valley Friends Meeting, wrote a *Proposed Earthcare Leading*:

> Friends endeavor to live joyfully, mindfully, and with reverent regard for the natural world, supporting one another and keeping this leading (care for the Earth and its natural systems) a discernible element of living in the manner of Friends.
>
> Cannon Valley Friends has endeavored to live in keeping with this leading and experience the rain garden as an extension of gathered worship.

She describes the process of creating the garden and why this was important:

> We wanted to practice our testimony of sustainability, even though our space was small. We decided we wanted the rain garden and we wanted to use native plants on the grounds as much as possible. We also wanted the rain garden to be a place of beauty and meditation.

The Meeting had several goals in mind:

> One goal was to provide a native area between our property and the neighbors rather than building a fence. Those bushes have grown well and now also provide the neighbor's chickens with some free range from time to time!

Another goal was to make it sustainable.

> We directed all of the drainage from the Meeting House roof to the garden. We also have a garage at the back of the property and did the same for the water from the garage. In addition, the back of our property is adjacent to the old Armory. We receive a lot of water from that roof, and made sure it was directed to the rain garden.

The garden also affirmed the Community testimony. Patricia says:

> [Creating it] was a great community event for us. One of our members made a lovely wood bench and the children made a peace pole for the

> garden. We have a birdhouse that usually has a resident wren.

Their rain garden also began to impact the neighborhood:

> A year ago, the house on our north side was torn down and a rather large apartment building was put in. The construction disrupted the garden and its peacefulness. The neighbors put up a fence and we are in the process of adjusting the plantings. Some of the apartments have balconies that overlook our yard, and we know some of the residents appreciate the garden. Once the rain garden was settled in, we discussed our front yard. We added a small native garden out there. We hope that those walking by see the beauty that the native plants provide and are encouraged to add more native plants to their own yards.

Some gardens are created partly as a result of a tragedy, such as the 2011 earthquake in Christchurch, New Zealand. The Christchurch Friends Meeting originally had a large gardens around their suburban Meeting house, but was forced to move to a more industrial city building after the earthquake.

Migs Eder, from the Christchurch Friends Meeting described this process:

> After an initial focus on earthquake-strengthening, we began work on the gardens. We gradually added a nut tree, peach, nectarine, quince, fig, pear, two apple trees, two grafted orange trees in tubs, blueberries, grapevines; and in three huge purpose-built wooden planters we have berries, currants, and strawberries. For the children, we have two tub gardens and two compost bins to demonstrate how pet worms create soil.

This garden also serves as community-building: the produce from the garden is being shared with members of the Meeting, and it's a place of meditation and reflection. Migs says:

> Our Wharenui (large/important house, usually translated as Meeting house) was so seriously institutional-looking that we felt compelled to add non-fruiting plants that are good for the soul, such as native New Zealand herbs. Nor can we overlook the development of the Lightwell garden, originally between two buildings until one was demolished post-earthquake. It is visible via a glass door from the main Meeting Room, and we've gradually transformed it into a green oasis.

Other Ways Quakers Practice Stewardship

The Stewardship Testimony also follows from the Quaker concern for social justice. We know that climate change and the destructiveness to Mother Nature can be traced, at least to some extent, to the human abuse of the gift of creation. We also know that the abuse of the environment unequally affects the poor, the disadvantaged, and Third World countries.

Care for the earth also means care for those who till the land, grow our food, and work to nourish our bodies. Workers have often been poor and at the mercy of the wealthy landowners.

John Woolman in the 1700s was already aware of this relationship. At that time, slaves were at the mercy of the slaveowners, but this relationship of the inequality between the poor and rich, the oppressed and the oppressors continues to our day. In *Conversations on the True Harmony of Mankind and How it May be Promoted*, Woolman sees "the relationship between the poor who till the land and the impoverishment of the land because of the desire for profit."

Woolman recognized how we destroy the Earth, a process that has become clearer in the twentieth and twenty-first centuries: "The products of the earth are a gift from our Gracious Creator to the inhabitants.

To impoverish the earth now to support outward greatness appears to be an injury to the succeeding age." Both wealthy and poor landowners overworked the soil and depleted the earth in the process.

The Philadelphia Yearly Meeting *Faith and Practice* book challenges us to reflect on these complex relationships between stewardship and social justice.[18]

> In today's world of economic interactions that are far more complex than when John Woolman lived, Friends are challenged to examine their decisions about money and other resources to see whether they contain not only the seeds of war, but also of self-indulgence, injustice, and ecological disaster. Good stewardship of economic resources consists both in avoiding these evils and acting to advance peace, simple living, justice and a healthy ecosystem. Good stewardship also requires attention to the needs of organizations that advance

> Friends' values, including our own meetings.
>
> Love for nature and care for our planet is part of our relationship with God. All of life is interconnected and when we neglect or abuse one part of it, we are causing disrepair in our relationship with what is divine and sacred. What we do to the natural world can benefit or harm. And so much of what we are doing now is close, or even past the point, of being irreparable in the damage it creates.[19]

Pacific Yearly Meeting, which is made up of Quaker Meetings from California, Hawaii, Nevada, and Mexico City, has written about these relationships, seeing our responsibility as a fundamental spiritual concern:

> From the beginning, it was through the wonders of nature that people saw God. How we treat the earth and its creatures is a basic part of our relationship with God. Our planet as a whole, not just the

> small parts of it in our immediate custody, requires our responsible attention.
>
> As Friends become aware of the interconnectedness of all life on this planet and the devastation caused by neglect of any part of it, we have become more willing to extend our sense of community to encompass all living things.

As Quakers, we not only have a responsibility to work for The Good for the Creation, we also have to be willing to look at ourselves individually as well as the collective responsibility of humanity. We are called to be realistic about the part we play in the destruction of our environment. Queries as well as studies about the reality of the dire danger that we are in as a planet, lead us to take these threats very seriously. When we work for social justice, we don't just look at the world objectively, but we also are willing to shine the light on the subjective side of stewardship. This is not a time in our history to avert our eyes from the role that we play.

Preparing The Next Generations

Friends' Colleges, such as Swarthmore College, Haverford College, Whittier College, Guilford College—as well as other colleges and universities—have courses on sustainability, stewardship, and environmental studies. Friends also have Quaker grade schools and high schools which teach children about the Testimonies and also encourages them to find innovative ways to apply the Testimonies. In the Portland Friends School in Portland, Maine, (preschool–8th grade), children are encouraged to present their ideas at board meetings. The newsletter from the school describes one of these interactions:

> Two eighth-grade students presented their ideas about how to reduce the plastic footprint at Friends School. One student proposed several ideas, including replacing plastic trash bags in classrooms with compostable alternatives and a further investigation into the role of synthetic chemicals in our cleaning

> products. Another student shared an action step of her Year-end Project, which included writing a grant through Eco Maine for a new dishwasher and dinnerware to discourage single-use plastics.
>
> Board members then worked collaboratively to keep these ideas moving forward. The science teacher, Nicole, clarified how these worked together as well as how impressed she was by her students' confidence: "For a small moment, we got to see what you hold as a board in terms of cost and logistics. And you got to see what we hold as a classroom and how passionate the students feel about this . . . You have to show the students that solutions are at our fingertips.

This school has a five-year vision which encourages imagining possibilities. The students are taught to identify and research an interest and then take action on that issue. Some of these issues include deforestation, Native American issues, and climate change, as well as teaching children to explore their surroundings and become more attuned to the natural world. They even encourage the children to become more comfortable with discomfort since this is what often pushes us to do more to help our world. Graduates of this school then continue to put what they have learned into practice. This leads some to go into the field of science or to use their knowledge of the natural world and translate it into the arts. Others go into education, teaching others to practice silent reflection so they can hear the guiding of the Spirit in their own lives and help make the world a better world.

Mary Tracy had these values in mind as a founding teacher of this school:

> The spiritual life of the school flourishes with the care of adults who are attuned to their own sense of awe and gratitude and grace, and pay attention to their own spiritual path. When that sense is present, we adults cannot help but notice the spiritual openness of

children, their easy connection to the natural world, and their ability to develop empathy. This means we listen carefully to children and reinforce their insights and sense of wonder. It means we provide time on a regular basis to be still, to reflect, to build awareness and compassion. It is not difficult—the world presents us with countless opportunities. We just have to open our eyes and ears.

The Holy Spirit Works in Nature

Many people who are spiritual see this commitment as a direct response to a recognition of the Holy Spirit's presence in nature. The poet, Elizabeth Barret Browning, says "Every common bush afire with God; but only he who sees, takes off his shoes—the rest sit round it and pick blackberries." We learn to see differently, expanding our consciousness and testing ourselves in terms of where we are in the challenge of this testimony.

Quaker poet, John Greenleaf Whittier (1807–1892), in his poem "The Worship of Nature"[20]:recognizes that we can either praise God or the Creation can be subdued and hurt by us:

The winds with hymns of praise are
 loud,
Or low with sobs of pain—
The thunder-organ of the cloud,
The dropping tears of rain.

With drooping head and branches
 crossed
The twilight forest grieves,
 Or speaks with tongues of
 Pentecost
From all its sunlit leaves.

The blue sky is the temple's arch,
Its transept earth and air,
The music of its starry march
The chorus of a prayer.

So Nature keeps the reverent frame
With which her years began,
And all her signs and voices shame
The prayerless heart of man.

We live with the reality that abuse of the Spirit can occur on every level of life. And we live with the faith and knowledge that the Holy Spirit cannot be subdued nor suppressed.

In my favorite poem, "God's Grandeur,"[21] poet Gerard Manley Hopkins (1844–1889), who was also a Catholic priest, recognizes that our imprint on the earth has compromised the Creation and yet, the Holy Spirit still reigns.

The world is charged with the grandeur of God.
It will flame out, like shining from shook foil;
It gathers to a greatness, like the ooze of oil
Crushed. Why do men then now not reck his rod?

Generations have trod, have trod,
have trod;
And all is seared with trade;
bleared, smeared with toil;
And wears man's smudge and
shares man's smell: the soil
Is bare now, nor can foot feel, being
shod.

And for all this, nature is never
spent;
There lives the dearest freshness
deep down things;
And though the last lights off the
black West went
Oh, morning, at the brown brink
eastward, springs—
Because the Holy Ghost over the
bent
World broods with warm breast
and with ah! bright wings.

The Spirit never gives up on any of us. Quakers, in unity with other religions, always hope to expand the Light Within, out into the world in its many manifestations.

All of these testimonies ask us to have faith in the Light—and in the potential effectiveness of our actions when we follow the Light given to us. Quakers are known for our attention to the inner workings necessary for us to respond to this Light. And we are known for the call to social justice. We try to bring the Light, that enlightens and guides us, ever outward, trying to do our part to create a kinder and more just world.

Queries about Stewardship

Do I see God and the Holy Spirit in nature?

How can I be a better steward of God's creation?

What do I do in my daily life to help the Creation, and how do I support issues and organizations that make our planet a better place?

Final Thoughts

In any faith tradition, one would hope that all the practices and rituals and nuances and resources would continue to transform a person throughout a lifetime. One would hope that the Holy Spirit is close and personal and that love and kindness and compassion and empathy would be enhanced as one grows into a relationship and even a union with the Holy Spirit. One would hope that the community embraces everyone, helps them in weakness and vulnerability, and values their strength and their contributions.

My experience growing into being a Quaker has been rich and fulfilling. And I hope that whatever path you take after reading this book, that this ever present and everlasting Light will be sweet and tender and uplifting. At the end of our journey, hopefully we have found the Light and it shines ever brighter.

If You'd Like to Read Further

If this book piqued your interest, there are wonderful books and other resources about Quakers you might enjoy.

Every Yearly Meeting has a *Faith and Practice* book which is updated about every ten to twenty years. You can find many of these online. These Yearly Meetings are made up of several states or several areas. You might want to look up the *Faith and Practice* book from Great Britian, New England, or the Intermountain Yearly Meeting, etc., which will give a brief history as well as explain many of our processes. They are also a good guide for Faith and Practice.

You might sign up for the American Friends Service Committee Newsletter, or subscribe to *Friends Journal* which is national in the United States, or some of the Friends bulletins and newsletters for certain areas. I occasionally write for the *Friends Journal* and the *Western Friends Journal* which includes California and most of the Western states.

If you want a good history of the Quakers, *Friends for 350 Years* by Howard H. Brinton and Margaret Hope Bacon is a wonderful resource and a very readable book. It has not been updated since 1974, but this book was given to me when I joined the Phoenix Friends Meeting and I found it such a good introduction.

Portrait in Gray: A Short History of the Quakers by John Punshon is another very good concise history of Quakers.

Mothers of Feminism by Margaret Hope Bacon is a wonderful history of how Quakers have contributed to the feminist movement, women's suffrage, and the equality of women. Some of the women you will recognize, such as Susan B. Anthony, but there are many unexpected surprises of women who were Quakers or were greatly influenced by Quakers. The first woman doctor—Dr. Elizabeth Blackwell—was helped by Quakers to get into medical school, which was a very long process. The first class that admitted women into medical school was made up of a very high percentage of Quaker women.

Many Quakers kept journals to reflect on their lives. Two of the best known are the *Journal of George Fox* and the *Journal of John Woolman*.

Two of my favorite books are *Prayer and Worship* and *Dimensions in Prayer* by Douglas Van Steere. I have read and reread these books for many, many years.

Other good books which combine Quakerism, history, and politics have been written by Elton Trueblood, Parker J. Palmer, and William Durland.

A Testament of Devotion by Thomas R. Kelly is considered a Quaker classic. It's very inspiring. Kelly's faith and love of God shines through every page.

Many Quaker meetings have good libraries. You can do an internet search for "Friends Meetings Near Me" and even small ones will probably have some good resources as well as people who will recommend others.

Final Query

You've heard what other Quakers say, but what do you say?

Do you feel moved, inspired, or transformed by issues and ideas in this book?

How is the Spirit leading you to help make you a better person and the world a better place?

Notes

1. *Presence in the Midst* by James Doyle Penrose, 1864.

2. https://www.bfs.org/apps/pages/AFriendsSchool. Accessed September 13, 2023.

3. http://www.quakercenter.org/programs/quaker-quote-archive/. Accessed September 13, 2023.

4. https://qfp.quaker.org.uk/passage/20-11/. Accessed October 4, 2023.

5. Searle, Stanford J. Jr., *The Meanings of Silence in Quaker Worship.* New York: The Edwin Mellen Press, 2005. pp38-39.]

6. Searle, Stanford J. Jr., *The Meanings of Silence in Quaker Worship.* New York: The Edwin Mellen Press, 2005. p 13.

7. http://www.perseus.tufts.edu/hopper/text?doc=Perseus%3Atext%3A2001.05.0313%3Achap-

ter%3D2%3Asection%3Dc.2.132. Accessed October 4, 2023.

8. Chestnut Hill Friends Meeting House, Philadelphia PA. "Skyspace" by Quaker James Turrell. Interior by James Bradbury, AIA, in collaboration with James Turrell. Photo by Quaker Terry Foss.

9. "The World Is Too Much With Us" by William Wordsworth (1770–1850).

10. *The Peaceable Kingdom* by Edwards Hicks (ca. 1833–1934).

11. Quakers before the judges of the Court of the English Court, United States. Colour engraving of the 19th century. / Photo © North Wind Pictures / Bridgeman Images.

12. Photo by Paul Henry. Photo used with permission.

13. "The Meaning of Membership," in *Searching the Depths: Essays on Being a Quaker Today*, edited by Harvey

Gillman and Alastair Heron, Quaker Home Service, 1996, pp. 72-76.

14. https://ny1.com/nyc/all-boroughs/news/2020/09/17/quaker-school-teachers-may-strike-over--union-busting--#:~:text=Brooklyn%20Quaker%20School%20Teachers%20May%20Strike%20Over%20'Union%20Busting'&text=NEW%20YORK%20%E2%80%94%20Brooklyn%20Friends%20School,set%20by%20the%20Trump%20administration. Accessed November 13, 2023.

15. Photo used with permission from Cannon Valley Friends Meeting.

16. https://renovare.org/articles/true-religion-of-the-inward-life. Accessed November 13, 2023.

17. Quaker Press, 2001

18. https://www.pym.org/faith-and-practice/faith-reflected-practice-daily-life/friends-witness-world/. Accessed November 15, 2023.

19. https://www.pym.org/earth-day-recommended-reads-youth-and-families/. Accessed November 15, 2023.

20. https://www.poetryfoundation.org/poems/45493/the-worship-of-nature. Accessed October 4, 2023.

21. https://www.poetryfoundation.org/poems/44395/gods-grandeur. Accessed October 4, 2023.

About the Author

Linda Seger, Th.D., is a theologian, author, speaker, and musician. She has been a Quaker (Society of Friends) since 1970. Throughout her 40-year career as a script consultant and seminar leader in the film industry she has applied her underlying Quaker practice to personal, professional, and spiritual fulfillment. She is the author of ten books on screenwriting and seven books on spirituality.

She attended Northwestern University where she received her M.A. in Drama, and went to seminary at Pacific School of Religion (M.A. in Religion and the Arts) and Graduate Theological Union (Th.D. in Drama and Theology).

Linda has received multiple book awards, including Illumination Book Awards, which shine a light on exemplary Christian books as well as awards for Christian Inspirational, Christian Living, Spirituality, and Meditation/Prayer. She lives in Cascade, Colorado with her sweetheart of a husband, Peter, and her magnificent cat, Tallinn. She zooms with the Portland, Maine daily and weekly Friends Meeting.

You can connect with Linda through her website: https://lindaseger.com/

Other Books by Dr. Linda Seger

Spirituality Books

Beyond Linear Thinking: Changing the Way We Live and Work

God's Part in Our Art: Making Friends with the Creative Spirit

Spiritual Steps on the Road to Success: Gaining the Goal Without Losing Your Soul

Jesus Rode a Donkey: Why Millions of Christians are Democrats

Reflections With God While Waiting to Be Healed

The Alphabet Prayer (co-written with Peter Le Var)

What Our Mamas Taught Us

Screenwriting and Film Books

Making a Good Script Great

Creating Unforgettable Characters

The Art of Adaptation:
Turning Fact and Fiction into Film

The Collaborative Art of Filmmaking: From Script to Screen (first two editions co-written with Edward Whetmore)

Making a Good Writer Great

When Women Call the Shots:
The Developing Power and Influence of Women in Television and Film

Advanced Screenwriting:
Taking Your Writing to the Academy Award Level

And the Best Screenplay Goes to . . .:
Learning from the Winners—Sideways, Shakespeare in Love, Crash

Writing Subtext: What Lies Beneath

You talkin' to me?: How to Write Great Dialogue (co-written with John Winston Rainey)

Made in United States
North Haven, CT
04 May 2024

52126207R00180